REV. FRANCIS R. DAVIS
ST. PATRICK'S CHURCH
274 DENISON PKWY. E.
CORNING, NEW YORK 14830-2995

The Words of Jesus

Arranged for Meditation with a Commentary
by Louis Michaels

TEMPLEGATE
Springfield, Illinois

© 1977 by Templegate
302 East Adams Street
P.O. Box 963
Springfield, Illinois 62705

All rights reserved, including the
right of reproduction in whole or in
part in any form.

SBN 87243-071-5

TABLE OF CONTENTS

Introduction 5

The Mission of Jesus 9

Tales of the Kingdom 49

The Heart of the Teaching 71

The Hard Sayings 99

As the Father Sent Me, So I Send You 111

Introduction

Jesus did not teach by words alone. The multiplication of the loaves and fishes, the cures he worked, the changing of water into wine and — most centrally — his death and resurrection, are all part of Jesus' teaching.

But the words of Jesus are essential to an understanding of his life and work, his death and resurrection. Here I have tried to present the teaching of Jesus in a somewhat different way, by offering his words in an arrangement which lends itself to reflection and meditation, with commentary which I hope will be helpful.

The order in which Jesus' words are given here is not that of scripture — the parables, for example, are gathered together into one section — and I have not included words which make sense only in the context of a particular action of Jesus, or which duplicate words already included. The intention of my arrangement is to relate the teachings, parables, and instructions of Jesus in new ways, which might allow them to take on fresh significance for the reader. This is also the reason for the use of a paraphrase (my own) rather than an existing translation. While there are some who argue that we already have too many translations and paraphrases, I think it can better be argued that we can never have enough. The more we see Jesus' message emphasized in new language, the better. A new phrasing can refresh the meaning of scripture, which all too often grows dull with repetition.

One thing I have *not* tried to do here is offer a substitute for the Gospels. The words of Jesus should first be met in context, and there is no way of distilling scripture, or offering it in capsule form. This book presumes a certain familiarity with the Gospels, and I hope that its effect will be to return you to the New Testament with new interest, rather than lead the reader away from it.

There are people who would reject the premise of this book on the grounds that the words of Jesus are not actually his words at all, but are instead the words of the evangelists, the recollection of his teachings by his first followers, and that it is therefore misleading to present them as Jesus' own. This case can be argued by one side, and just as vehemently denied on the other by some fundamentalists. But without entering the argument on either side I think it can be said that the presentation of these words as Jesus' own is more significant than anything else. The fact that the evangelists ascribed these words to Jesus, to the one who was with the Father before time began, who became human to save us, and rose to show us the glory which is our destiny — that fact gives these words much more than ordinary importance, even more than ordinary scriptural importance. In these words you can expect to find Christianity's center, the core beliefs which are involved in following what was often called "the New Way" upon its first appearance.

I hope that this arrangement of Jesus' words, along with the commentary which has been added to set a context or underscore a theme, will serve to illuminate the fact that these words are spoken to each one of us, and are meant to take flesh in us, so that we may be counted as his followers, and finally as part of that risen family of which he was the first-born.

— Louis Michaels

The Mission of Jesus

The teaching of Jesus, and what he expects of his followers, cannot be separated from Jesus himself. It all begins with him. The person of Jesus, and what Christianity has claimed about him, is what makes Christianity unique. What we have come to call Christian ethics can be found in Judaism and among the Greek stoics. Other religions have known prayer, mysticism, sacrifice, a belief in one God; only Christianity claims that a particular man, Jesus Christ, was both fully human and fully divine. He was fully human: he knew pain, loneliness, despair, as well as friendship, the taste of bread, fish, wine, and honey. And he was divine: he knew that he stood in a special relationship to his Father, and we read that he was aware of this relationship at an early age. When his parents looked for him in the temple, he asked "Why have you looked for me? Don't you know that I must be about my Father's business?" (Luke 2:49) Later, when he had begun his preaching and healing mission, he was asked who he was, and answered, "I am what I have told you from the start. There is much I have to say about you, and much judgement too. But the one who sent me is truthful, and what he tells me is what I tell the world." (John 8:25-26) This identification of himself with the will of God is the most startling claim made for Jesus — it disturbs us precisely because it is the claim made throughout history by fanatics and madmen. As C. S. Lewis and other writers have pointed out, Jesus was either who his followers said he was, or he was mad, or he was a wicked liar, wicked because he claimed what no man can claim without committing the ultimate blasphemy.

There is another view, one which is popular with many people today. It recognizes the value of many Christian teachings, but says that Jesus' followers made a god of him after his death. They turned a simple ethical teacher, a Jewish reformer, into a deity; in doing so they betrayed the simple ethics which was the basis of his teaching. Frequently this transformation of Jesus from an ethical itinerant rabbi with reformist leanings into a God-man is blamed on St. Paul.

The problem with this view is the unanimity, not only of scripture, but of the entire early church. Even the Judaizing parties within the early church insisted that Jesus was the fulfillment of Israel's messianic hopes, and Paul's message was not considered radically different from that of other Christian teachers. There was some opposition in Jerusalem to Paul's belief that the whole Jewish law should not be imposed on Gentile converts, and that it was not absolutely binding on Jews; but this opposition was overcome with less vehemence than would have been required if Paul was doing the radical surgery he has been accused of doing. The difficulty with claiming that Jesus' message was radically transformed by the early church is that there is no evidence for the claim. It means saying that the words attributed to Jesus in the New Testament bear no relationship at all to the words he actually spoke; it means saying that his followers completely misunderstood the man. All of which, of course, is simply asserted. The reason for making the assertion brings us back to the problem of Jesus himself: it is a way of trying to avoid serious consideration of the claim made by Christians that "the Word became flesh, and lived with us." That is the difficult but absolutely central claim of Christianity.

The gospels are not, however, simple history. They were written down a generation after Jesus, and were not intended as journalistic accounts. They were presentations of his person and teaching, done for those to whom the good news was still a very new and fresh thing. We should, in reading the New Testament, try to enter into the spirit of someone hearing the word for the first time. And this is not play-acting . . . we may be making a great mistake if we believe that the Jesus we have heard about all of our lives is the true Jesus, the one who asks to become Lord of our life, and our greatest servant. Sometimes we have heard the words so often they are nearly meaningless, and sound like consoling cliches. It is this familiarity which we have to overcome to hear the Word fresh, as its first hearers did.

One step towards overcoming our familiarity is to consider what it means to say that Jesus was truly human, as well as truly divine. By emphasizing the divine we may make ourselves too distant from the human Jesus — which is to say, from the only point at which we can honestly begin to understand him, even in his divine aspect. Jesus was not a god who looked like a man (as some Christians seem to present him). He was fully human; if not, his humanity was a trick, an educational device. Christians insisted on this real humanity from the beginning. The pain of the cross was real pain, and the feeling of abandonment was real abandonment.

The paradox of Christianity is that by going to the depths of his humanity Jesus' followers can see his divinity revealed.

We read that at the beginning of his career Jesus took his place among sinners to receive the baptism of John. In Matthew's gospel we hear John protesting, and Jesus answers "Let it be so for now. It is good for us to fulfill everything which righteousness demands." (Matthew 3:15)

If we read this too carelessly we might assume that Jesus did this simply to set a good example. But Mark's gospel tells the same story in a stark way: Jesus receives John's baptism, and the heavens open for the descent of the Spirit. He retires to the wilderness to pray and fast — and we have to wonder whether until that time he had any idea that his life was to be marked off so radically from other lives. We see him next after John's arrest, taking up John's message: "Repent — the Kingdom of God is at hand!" He took up the life of a wanderer: "The foxes have holes," he said, "and the birds of the air have nests, but the Son of Man has nowhere to lay his head." (Matthew 8:20)

The wandering life which Jesus undertook involved healing; this was not only the healing of the body, but the healing forgiveness brings. When confronted with the adulterous woman, he said, after revealing the sins of her accusers, "No one condemns you? Then neither do I: Go, and do not sin again." (John 8:10-11) This compassion was not only for the terribly maimed or sinful people; it showed itself in more common ways, as common as bread: "I have compassion for the crowds. They have been with me for three days and have eaten nothing. If I send them home hungry, some may grow faint along the way." (Mark 8:2-3)

We must realize, in order to see Jesus with new eyes, that this compassion, this sense of vocation, was not only a movement of God's will towards us, though it was that. It was also a man's genuine compassion and deep feeling for his brothers and sisters — that is, us. One of the lessons he teaches us is that at the depths of the most human feelings and the most common kinds of love there is something of God's compassion.

THE COMING OF THE KINGDOM: JOHN THE BAPTIST

John was a prophet, a wild man who came out of the desert, preaching that the Kingdom of God was at hand — the deliverance for which the world had been waiting was about to make itself seen. He called the crowds to repentance, baptizing them as a symbol of the radical change they were willing to make in their lives. He was popular — not with the religious establishment, which considered him an embarrassment, but with the poor and socially unrespectable.

John recognized Jesus as the fulfillment of the people's hopes. Referring to Jesus, he said, "He must become greater, and I must become less." When John was imprisoned Jesus began his own preaching, which must have looked to many as a simple continuation of John's: "Repent," Jesus said. "The Kingdom of God is at hand." Now Palestine was occupied by Roman troops, with a Roman governor, and a constant Roman suspicion of the Jews, who had never allowed themselves to be assimilated as easily as other conquered peoples. The political situation was highly charged, and preaching a new kingdom made religious and political leaders uneasy. This uneasiness probably contributed to John's imprisonment (though his condemnation of the king for an illicit marriage was the excuse).

Throughout his preaching Jesus referred to John, often with powerful affection and respect; at times he seems to burn with hatred for those responsible for John's imprisonment and martyrdom. John at one point appears to have been puzzled by Jesus, and sent his disciples to ask if Jesus was the one they had been waiting for. Jesus did not answer with a simple yes or no:

> **Go and tell John the things you have seen and heard — how the blind see, the lame walk, lepers are healed, the deaf hear, the dead are raised, and the poor have good news told to them. Blessed is the one who does not take offense at me.**
> — Matthew 11:4-6

Jesus points to the signs of the kingdom, which is not to be political; it shows itself in the deeper levels of healing, compassion, and justice. (Note that the poor hearing good news is considered as marvelous as the healing of lepers and sight for the blind!)

Jesus revealed his great admiration for John when he asked the crowd:

> When you went out into the desert, what did you expect to see? A reed shaken in the wind? What was it you went to see? A man dressed in fine clothes? But you must go to king's courts to find people who dress well and live soft lives.
> So what was it you went to see? A prophet? Yes — but I tell you he is much more than a prophet. This is the one of whom scripture says "I send my messenger before your face; he will prepare your way before you."
> I tell you that no greater prophet has ever been born of woman than John the Baptist. But the least person in the Kingdom of God is even greater. — Luke 7:24-28

There is something caustic about Jesus' words to the crowd here. He challenges our tendency to look for comfort and ease in religion, contrasting it with John's stark, single-hearted dedication to God's message. John is the last and greatest prophet, Jesus says, the herald preceding the kingdom of God. And God's kingdom is so full a reality that even the greatest prophet is dwarfed in comparison with those lucky enough to participate in its coming.

> What comparison can I make that fits this generation? What are they like? They are like children who sit in the marketplace, calling to each other, "When we piped to you, you would not dance; when we wailed for you, you would not weep." When John the Baptist came, not eating bread or drinking wine, you said "He is possessed." The Son of Man comes eating and drinking, and you say "Look, a glutton, a drinker! A friend of tax collectors and sinners!" But the truth of God's wisdom is proved by her children. — Luke 7:31-35

> Elias truly will come first and restore all things. But I tell you: Elias has already come, and they had their way with him. In the same way they will make the Son of Man suffer. — Matthew 17:11-12

Once Jesus' enemies, trying to trap him into speaking blasphemy, asked him how he came by his authority — who gave it to him? Jesus answered, "Let me ask you a question in return, and if you answer, I will answer your question. Was John's baptism from God, or was it merely a human thing?" This caused some consternation: John was popular with many of the people, and to say that it was merely human would lead them to reject their leaders. But to say that it was from God, when they themselves had rejected John, would make them look like those who had resisted prophets throughout history. They refused to answer, and Jesus continued:

Since you can't answer, I will not tell you by what authority I do these things. But let me ask you this: A certain man had two sons. He came to the first and said, "Son, work in my vineyard today." The son answered, "I will not." But after awhile he repented, and went.
He went to the second son and asked him to work as well. He answered, "I'll go right away!" — but he did not.
Which of the two did the will of the Father?
I tell you, tax collectors and whores go into the kingdom of God before you do. John came to you for the sake of the truth, and you did not believe him. But tax collectors and whores believed him. Even when you saw this you did not repent and believe him. — Matthew 21:23-32

If I am the only one to be a witness on my own behalf, my witness would not be true; but another is my witness, and I know that his witness on my behalf is true. You asked John, and he bore witness to the truth. (Not that I need any man's witness — I have told you these things for your own good, for your salvation.) He was like a light, burning and shining, and you were willing to enjoy his light — for awhile. But I have a greater witness than John: the works which the Father has given me to bring to completion, the works I am doing, these witness to the fact that the Father has sent me. — John 5:31-36

THE BEGINNING OF JESUS' WORK

The gospels of Matthew, Mark, and Luke tell us that after he had received John's baptism of repentance Jesus went into the desert. Before going out to the people he had to spend time in solitude, where he fasted and prayed for forty days. The forty days correspond to the forty years of Israel's trial in the desert, and this connection with the time of testing which the Jews faced in Moses' time — a time which ended in their gaining the promised land — is brought here to a personal level by Jesus, who endures this trial before beginning his mission, a mission which manifested the Kingdom of God which is within each one of us. We read that during his time in the desert he was tempted. Mark simply mentions this and goes on, while Matthew and Luke provide an account of temptation which reveals the ancient roots of Jesus' struggle, and his mission; they also show what was new about it. Jesus was tempted to a wordly, material security; he was asked to show his power over God; he was tempted to political power. When Satan asks Jesus to turn stones to bread he answers:

It is written, "Man shall not live by bread alone, but by every word which proceeds from the mouth of God."

When Jesus is asked to cast himself from the temple, forcing angels to rescue him, he tells Satan:

It is written, "You shall not tempt the Lord, your God."

And when Satan shows him the nations of the world, saying that he will give Jesus the same power he, Satan, has over them, if Jesus will adore him, Jesus answers:

Leave, Satan. It is written, "You shall worship the Lord, your God, and you shall serve him alone. — Matthew 4:4-10

All of the answers which Jesus gives to Satan are taken from Deuteronomy (the sixth and the eighth chapters), showing Jesus' fidelity to the law. But in addition the answers show something of the character of his mission. It is not to be associated with power or merely with material needs; nor is it to be based on spectacular displays of divine power. This almost self-effacing character is given by Jesus to his work from the beginning of his mission; it points away from him to the Father and the Father's work — with which Jesus is nevertheless identified. This humility is something which is also to be applied to his followers. Later he will point out that their way is not to be like that of the rulers of the world; they are to serve rather than be served, and simple justice and charity are to be considered signs of the kingdom rather than miraculous events or political dominance. This is the beginning of his paradoxical message: it is his humility and servanthood which show his relationship to the ruler of the universe, and his followers will similarly show their participation in his divine life by emptying themselves of divine ambitions. Just as Moses showed the wandering Israelites the kingdom which had been promised to them, Jesus opens the way to a kingdom which stakes itself out in our hearts.

But it is not without exterior consequences, as Jesus later makes clear in quoting Isaiah:

> The Spirit of the Lord is upon me, because he has anointed me to bring good news to the poor. He has sent me to heal the broken-hearted, to preach freedom to captives, and sight to the blind, to free those who are oppressed, and to proclaim a year of the Lord's favor . . . Today this scripture is fulfilled, just as you hear it.
> — Luke 4:18-19,21

Jesus made it clear that his mission was not to conventionally religious, self-righteous, or moralistic believers. Even the law, holy as it is, is a means to an end — and one of its ends is to serve the real needs of human beings.

> Haven't you read what David did, when he and his men were hungry? How he went into the house of God when Abiathar was high priest and ate the holy bread, which only the priests were allowed to eat, and shared it with his companions? The sabbath was made for people — people were not made for the sabbath. So the Son of Man is Lord of the sabbath.
> — Mark 2:25-28

> Those who are whole do not need a doctor, but those who are sick do. Go learn what this means: I want mercy, not ritual. I have not come to call good people, but sinners, to repent.
> — Matthew 9:12-13

His work was the beginning of something new — but it answered a need as old as history.

> Happy are the eyes who see the things you see. I tell you, many prophets and kings wanted to see what you see, and did not see; they wanted to hear the things you hear, and did not hear them.
> — Luke 10:23-24

THE HEALING WORK OF JESUS

The most startling aspect of Jesus' mission is the power he revealed in healing those in misery. Along with the resurrection it has sometimes been mentioned as a proof of his divinity (although it is clear from scripture that faith is necessary to see this; and if there must be a prior faith, miracles can't be considered proofs in the ordinary sense).

How should we see them? First of all, with wonder. The fact that we have heard these stories over and over again can lead us to overlook the wonder which his healing power must have evoked in those who first encountered it. These works were the first signs that the Kingdom was coming. In C. S. Lewis' *The Lion, the Witch, and the Wardrobe*, the coming of Aslan, a wonderful liberating lion, frees a world which has been bewitched. This terrible enchantment is represented as a deep winter with no thaw; and the witch who has held the world in her grip is terrified at the signs of the thaw and the oncoming spring.

Jesus' works can be seen this way: they were signs of spring. Demons are represented as terrified of him, and his attitude towards them is one of anger. He is moved with compassion, first, for the one who suffers, and then with anger at the demon who causes the suffering. One of the most chilling of the stories the gospels tell of demonic possession is of the young man who lived among tombs, whose demon is asked by Jesus, "What is your name?" (It was thought in ancient times that to know someone's name was to have power over him.) "Legion," he answers — "A swarm," in other words. These demons are seen to be not only in charge, but tormented. Not only the young man, but the world itself is seen to be in the grip of a power which is dark, dismal, and miserable. Before Jesus this power dwindles to nothing. Evil's force vanishes before the power and goodness of God, and at the end of the story the disciples find the young man, clean and clothed now, sitting at Jesus' feet.

Jesus' healing is a sign of the compassion his father feels towards all who suffer, a compassion so great that it includes the servant of the high priest who comes to take him to his death. When the servant is wounded by one of Jesus' followers, Jesus heals him. Seen at one level, his acts remind us of magic, and this impression is reinforced by the incident described in the eighth chapter of Luke. A woman who had suffered for years believes that if she touches only the fringe of Jesus' robe she will be healed, and as she touches it he asks, "Who touched me? Someone has touched me — I can tell that power has gone out of me!" When the woman is brought forth, trembling, he consoles her: "Be comforted, daughter. Your faith has made you whole. Go in peace."

If we stop at the notion that Jesus was filled with a kind of electric charge which was in some sense beyond his control we make his power magic. The point of the story is deeper: it is the faith of the woman which makes the miracle possible, which seems even to control Jesus' power. This picture of a compassion which, in a sense, cannot control itself but must go forth to the sufferer is surprising, and appealing as well. It reminds us of Jesus' story of the unjust judge who responds to the complaining plaintiff: if even an unjust person responds so readily, how much more will God listen. He also compares God's love to the love of fathers who give their children food as soon as they are asked, and not stones or serpents in place of bread and fish. Jesus' miracles must be seen as signs of God's overflowing generosity. They are to be seen in the context of his mission to us, as signs of God's kingdom and its coming; they reveal the necessity of faith, and also the necessity of witnessing to that faith; and finally they give us a glimpse of Jesus' relationship to his Father.

When Jesus released people from physical ailments, or from the forces of evil which bound them, he frequently connected this evil with the forgiveness of sin. In our culture we have divided evil into categories: there is natural evil (like death, madness, earthquakes and famine), human evil (like deliberate unkindness, greed and sin), and complications which result from human evil on a large scale (war, poverty and oppression). In the New Testament these are not radically separated; they are seen as belonging to the same general category, an evil which has as a distinguishing characteristic the destruction it works on human life. Whether it is illness or sin, it makes people suffer. It is a matter of degree, not a difference in kind. Of course Jesus regarded sin as the greatest evil. Sin is what separates people from God, and it can be healed only at the deepest level — the level of the heart. It is an even deeper wound than illness. When Jesus encountered a young man who was paralyzed he told him first, "Son, your sins are forgiven." When reproached for his obvious blasphemy he responded with a more obvious sign, but one which showed at a lesser level the depth of his power, in terms too obvious to ignore or dispute.

Why do you worry over these things? Which would you find easier — to say to someone paralyzed "Your sins are forgiven?" Or to say

"Get up, take your cot with you and walk?" In order to show that the Son of Man has power on earth to forgive sins, I tell you: rise, take your cot, and go home.
— Mark 2:5-12

Frequently Jesus' miracles are placed against a background of narrow incomprehension. The usual attitude towards sin and forgiveness, towards illness and healing, is cramped and small compared with the generosity which God would show if given the opening. In this context Jesus' statements, beginning "Which is easier?" or "Is it lawful?" are like taunts; they could almost be seen as signs of desperation.

Is it lawful to do good on the sabbath, or to do evil? To save life, or to kill it?
— Mark 3:4

Hypocrites! Even on the sabbath, isn't it true that you each release your ox or donkey from the stall and take him out to the water? Shouldn't this woman — a daughter of Abraham! — who has been bound by Satan for fully eighteen years be let loose from her bond on this sabbath day?
—Luke 13:15-16

Is it lawful to heal on the sabbath? Is there any one of you who, if his donkey or ox falls into a ditch, will not pull him out immediately, even on the sabbath?
— Luke 14:3-5

The wholeness of physical healing is only the beginning, a sign of a deeper need.

Now you are made whole. Do not sin any more; something worse happens as a result.
— John 5:14

This is not a threat — rather, the cure which Jesus worked should not be taken with indifference, but should be received with gratitude. That gratitude leads to a changed life — at the personal level a turning towards God, away from sin; and where life is shared with others, a commitment to witness to the power of God.

I want to you to be healed . . . Now do not tell anyone about this;

instead, go and show yourself to the priest, and offer the gift that Moses required, as a testimony to them. — Matthew 8:3-4

Go home to your friends — tell them that the Lord has done great things for you, and has shown you compassion. — Mark 5:19

Faith was necessary for Jesus' work; even the power of God at work in him could not work against our will. But this faith is not always the kind that moves mountains. One of the most encouraging stories, for us of little faith, is the one in which the grieving father, asked if he believes, replies, "I believe — but help my lack of belief!" This is sufficient. Belief in the power of God to change things is the context for every cure Jesus worked. It is a kind of refrain:

Go your way — your faith has made you whole. — Mark 10:52

Daughter, it is your faith which has made you whole. Go in peace, cured of your disease. — Mark 5:34

Do you believe that I am able to do this? According to your faith, may it be done. See that no one knows about it.
 — Matthew 9:28-30

Be comforted: your faith has made you whole. — Matthew 9:22

Go your way. Because you have believed, it will be done.
 — Matthew 8:13

What would you like me to do for you? Receive your sight: your faith has saved you. — Luke 18:41-42

The lack of faith which he encountered so frequently frustrated Jesus — but even here he acted with compassion; when his disciples were unable to help someone believed to be possessed he showed his irritation — and helped the victim.

You faithless generation! How long must I be with you? How long must I endure you? Bring him here to me.
— Mark 9:19

Jesus made it clear that his mission was to the house of Israel — but Gentiles were not excluded. In fact, it is made clear that their inclusion was a central part of his mission. One of the most curious passages in the gospel — because of its apparent harshness — is the answer of Jesus to the Gentile woman who asked him to cure her daughter.

Let the children eat their fill first. It would not be right to take the bread of children and throw it to dogs.
— Mark 7:27

When the woman replied that even dogs have a right to eat the food which falls under the table, Jesus answered her request.

Because of what you have said, go your way — the devil has left your daughter.
— Mark 7:27-29

Jesus' harsh answer to the woman's request is met with wit, with a humor which seems even brash to us — there are few people in the New Testament who respond to Jesus this way (or, it might be said, who have occasion to answer him in this manner). The fact that she is undaunted, that she pursues her request, is a sign of her faith. Her humor and her quickness may also be signs. In any case, Jesus responds by moving from what looks like an exclusive mission to one which includes "outsiders". This is the main point of the story: it is faith, not any kind of membership, which opens the doors of the kingdom. Jesus' usual response to Gentiles is not exclusive — this story may be intended by its extreme character to underscore the point — but rather shows that the Kingdom of God is universal. This is shown in many places — especially the parable of the good Samaritan. There are other Samaritans in the gospels, one of them a leper cured by Jesus, one of ten who was cured, and the only grateful one.

Weren't ten men cured? Where are the other nine? Only this stranger returned to give glory to God. Rise, go your way: your faith has made you whole.
— Luke 17:17-19

When a Gentile soldier asked Jesus to cure his sick servant, Jesus was about to leave for the soldier's house to help him. But the soldier said that he understood what it was to have a little authority, and surely the authority of Jesus was such that he did not need to go all the way to the servant's bedside — his word would be enough. Jesus responded to this simplicity:

Truly, I tell you that I have not found faith as great as this in all of Israel. I tell you, many will come from east and west and will sit down in company with Abraham, Isaac, and Jacob in the kingdom of heaven. But the children of the kingdom will be thrown into the darkness outside, where there will be weeping and the grinding of teeth.

— Matthew 8:10-12

Many passages of the New Testament have been interpreted in a way which is, putting it bluntly, anti-Semitic. Among them are the passages which refer to the children of the kingdom (and other phrases used to signify Israel) being cast out, while strangers will be brought in. But there is a problem with this: it is unlikely that Jesus would have bothered to go to all this trouble simply to challenge a first century Palestinian religious establishment. The lesson the churches must learn from these passages are ones which apply to every religious establishment, every organization which claims to speak God's truth in any degree. Where any church settles for a comfortable or consoling, smug or legalistic way of speaking about the living God, Jesus' judgements apply.

Faith is essential. It is not enough to say that you are a follower of Jesus to be counted as faithful. When Jesus cured a boy his followers were unable to cure, they asked him why they were unable to cast out the devil in this case. Jesus answered:

Because of your lack of faith. I tell you truthfully that if you had faith as small as a grain of mustard seed, you could say to this mountain, "Go from here to there," and it would go; nothing would be impossible for you. But the only way to cast this sort out is by prayer and fasting.
— Matthew 17:14-21

It was commonly believed that people suffered physical agony because of sins they or their parents had committed. Jesus was asked of a man who was blind from birth whether he or his parents had sinned.

It is not that this man has sinned, or his parents; he is this way so that God's works can be made manifest in him. I must do the works of the one who sent me while daylight lasts — the night comes soon, when no one can work. As long as I am in the world, I am the light of the world.
— John 9:3-5

The gospel tells us that Jesus raised people from the dead. He raised the son of a widow, telling her, "Don't cry." He brought the daughter of a leader of the synagogue to life, speaking gently to her and asking that food be brought to her when she awakened. These examples of his tenderness, combined with his power, appear most strongly in the story of Lazarus. Jesus said of Lazarus' death, "This sickness does not end in death, but is for God's glory, to give glory to the Son of God." When he told his followers, "Our friend Lazarus is asleep; I will go, to awaken him from sleep," they did not understand. He spoke plainly then, telling them that Lazarus was dead, and went to the place of his burial because his friends Mary and Martha had asked him to come. He told Martha:

Your brother will rise again.

She must have thought this was simple piety — as a good Pharisee she answered, "Of course he will, on resurrection day." Then Jesus said:

I am the resurrection and the life. He who believes in me, even if death takes him, will live. Whoever lives and believes in me will not die. Do you believe this?

Martha answered "I believe that you are the anointed one, the Son of God, who was meant to come." When Jesus joined the mourners who were to accompany Martha and Mary to the tomb he asked, "Where have you buried him?" At the sight of their tears he was deeply troubled. He wept. And then on arriving at the tomb he said,

Take away the stone.
Didn't I tell you that if you believed you would see the glory of God?

> Father, I thank you for hearing me.
> I know that you always hear me — I have said this before the people so that they may believe that you have sent me.
> Lazarus, come forth!
>
> — John 11

We are told that he said this with a loud voice. We are also told that Lazarus did come forth, wrapped in his burial clothes, and that Jesus asked the people to unwind the winding cloths to free him.

What are we to make of these tales of resurrection? Are they simply forerunners of Jesus' own rising from the dead? Not quite. The people involved lived normal lives, and eventually died. But Jesus' resurrection did not end in death. These tales are signs of Jesus' power — clearly divine, if it could extend even over death! But in the story of Lazarus there are added depths. In the gospel of John the confession of faith in Jesus as the Son of God has happened before. After his cure of the man born blind, the man seeks out Jesus after having been rejected by those who would not believe his honest story of his cure (or perhaps they were afraid to believe), and Jesus asks him, "Do you believe in the Son of God?" The man answers, "Who is he, Lord, so that I can believe in him?" Jesus responds, "You have seen him — it is the one you are talking to!" And the man, saying "Lord, I believe," worships him.

But this confession of faith follows a cure. Jesus puts the same question to Martha as she grieves. The miracle has not been accomplished; she is probably, at the time of the question, not at all sure what Jesus has in mind. Even though Jesus knows that God's power will soon raise Lazarus, Martha does not — and still she makes her confession of faith.

This seems to me to be the beginning of a truly Christian attitude towards death. It is frequently presented to us as an easy thing for Christians. They believe in life everlasting and resurrection from the dead — why should they face it with fear and anguish? But here we have to remember that there are few places in the gospel where we are given any clue about Jesus' own emotions. One is in the passages which describe the agony in the garden of Gethsemane, just before his own death. It was agonizing for him, we are told. Another is at this place — the story of Lazarus. The mourning of his friends and the depth of their sorrow, make Jesus himself weep. In the face of his sadness and fear it seems callous and shallow to make death a light thing. No Christian should expect to have it easier than Jesus did.

These works of Jesus — all of them, all the miracles of healing and exorcism and even raising the dead — must be seen as his victory over every evil possibility. The greatest healing of all was the forgiveness of sin. It shows how jaded we are, that we think of it as the least spectacular.

JESUS THE PROPHET

A prophet is not without honor — except in his own country, among his family, and in his own house.
— Mark 6:4

I tell you the truth: no prophet is accepted in his own country. There were many widows in Israel during Elijah's time, when the skies were closed tight for three years and six months and there was a great famine everywhere in the country. But Elijah was not sent to any of them, but to Sarepta, in Sidon, to a widow who lived there. And there were many lepers in Israel at the time of Elisha the prophet, but none of them was cured, except Naaman — a Syrian.
— Luke 4:24-27

How can you talk about having no bread? Don't you see? Don't you understand? Are your hearts still hard? You have eyes — are you blind? You have ears — are you deaf? Don't you remember? When I broke five loaves among five thousand people, how many baskets full of fragments did you collect? Why is it that you can't understand?
— Mark 8:17-21

The prophets were upsetting to any group of people who believed they knew the will of God. They showed that God was stranger than the people ever imagined him to be. Because of the upset they caused (upsetting was, you can almost say, part of their job) they were frequently rejected. The Old Testament is full of examples of people who accepted the prophets — widows, children, outcasts, and foreigners, people despised by the respectable and safe, precisely because of their need. Today we have different classes of despised people. Some are willing to shut the old away, or laugh at the unlettered, or find themselves superior to the poor men and women on skid row. Some of these people are the surprising heroes of the Bible, the ones who accepted the prophets despised by the respectable.

Elijah the prophet was given hospitality by a widow, and in return he made sure that her flask of oil and store of flour remained full. This miracle is very much like the multiplication of the loaves and fishes which Jesus worked, announcing the immediate presence of God's power just as the prophets did frequently, from Moses and Aaron onward — by manifesting it in a startling sign, a sign which revealed God's power and, frequently, his generosity. In the face of this, the small-mindedness of the people God tries again and again to reach stands out in sharp contrast.

When Jesus speaks of the prophet who lives without honor among those who should know him best, our first response is to sympathize with the loneliness of his situation. It is a false response. We have been given clues to the end of the mystery all our lives — *we* know him, we tell ourselves; *we* would honor him; but this is based on the fact that we know the story. How — if we were faced first-hand with the need to make the right decision — would we respond? We would not by encountering "Jesus Christ", a name we have come to know far too well. We would be meeting a new name, the name of a person distrusted, even hated, by most of the people we have been taught to revere. His appeal to the disreputable would appear shocking. We have to remember that the disreputable here were not just prostitutes and poor beggars; they were profiteering businessmen like Zaccheus and people who collected taxes for the despised Roman occupation forces. It is as if Jesus numbered among his friends whores and society ladies, Richard Nixon and Daniel Ellsberg, the head of the local Black Panther Party and the head of the local office of the FBI. This reconciliation was not simple tolerance — he made it clear that his followers were to be wholeheartedly dedicated to a new way of living which would not include their former allegiances. But it was his insistence, and that of his first followers, that the Kingdom could exclude no one on the grounds of race or class or some notion of respectability.

Every kingdom divided against itself falls into ruin. A divided household falls. So if Satan is divided against himself how will his kingdom stand? You tell me that my power to cast out devils comes from Beelzebub — but if it is by Beelzebub that I cast out devils, how do your own people cast them out? Let them be your judges. But if it is by God's finger that I cast out devils, then you can be sure that the Kingdom of God is now in your presence.

When a well-armed man guards his palace, everything he owns is safe. But when somebody stronger comes, and defeats him, he takes all of the weapons he trusted away from him, and divides up the spoils.

He who is not with me is against me. He who does not gather with me scatters.

When the unclean spirit leaves a man, he walks through deserts looking for rest, and when he finds no resting place he says, "I will return to the house I left." When he has returned he finds it freshened up and cleaned. So he goes off to find seven other spirits more wicked than he is, and they all come in and live there, and in the end that man is worse than he was at first.

— Luke 11:17-26

The miracles worked by Jesus were signs of the reconciliation of God's work with human work, a reconciliation in the divine and human nature of Jesus which was the first sign of the Kingdom he brought to birth. As such they were attacks upon the power of evil. The critical nature of his mission is emphasized by the "either/or" implication of the words, "He who is not with me is against me." No neutrality or indifference is possible in this battle between good and evil. Perhaps this is part of the meaning of the story about the demon who returns to the home he has left. It has been freshly cleaned — and at the same time it is empty. There is room for demons there. It is this emptiness, this lack of attention, against which we are cautioned.

I have food to eat that you do not know about. My food is to do the will of the one who sent me, and finish the work he began.

Don't you say, "There are four months left until harvest time"? I tell you, if you would look up you could see that the hills are already full and white for the harvest. The one who reaps is gathering crops for eternal life, so that the one who sows and the one who reaps may rejoice together. This is how the saying is proved true: "One sows, another reaps." I sent you to reap that which you did not work for. Other men worked, and you have entered their work to complete it.

— John 4:32-38

When Jesus says that his life comes from doing the work of the Father, and goes on to say that the one who sows and the one who reaps will rejoice together, he puts his whole vocation on earth in a few words. He has begun to gather the crops his Father sowed through all the prophets who came before Jesus, and his followers are his co-workers. The joy the Father shares with the Son is shared with those who are the Son's followers.

You do not know what spirit rules you. The Son of Man has not come to destroy lives, but to save them. — Luke 9:55-56

This is the answer that Jesus gave his followers when they wanted to call fire from heaven down on people who rejected them. The same spirit shows in his tender request for Zacchaeus' hospitality, made in the face of the common disdain shown to the man because "he was a sinner."

Zacchaeus, hurry and come down. Today I have to visit your house.
Today salvation has come to this house, because this man is also one of Abraham's children. The Son of Man has come to search for and save what was lost. — Luke 19:5,9-10

This is another case of Jesus revealing one of the mysteries of the Kingdom of God: that God offers so much more than we expect. Zacchaeus wanted only a glimpse of Jesus, who surprised and delighted him by asking to be his guest. There are indications throughout the gospels that a spirit of joy surrounded Jesus and his friends.

Can the members of the wedding party fast, when the bridegroom is with them? Of course they can't, while the bridegroom is with them. But there will come days when the bridegroom will be taken from them, and they will fast in those days.
No one sews a piece of new cloth onto an old garment; the new piece will shrink and tear the old cloth, making the tear a worse one. No one puts new wine into old wineskins; the new wine, fermenting, will tear the old skins, the wine will spill and the skins will be ruined. New wine calls for new wineskins. — Mark 2:19-22

The news brought by Jesus is new — but it is built on the old. This dialogue between the new and old, both of them seen as unique and necessary, is repeated elsewhere in the words about the good steward who can bring from his storehouse new and old things both. In

Revelations the voice from the throne says, "Behold, I make all things new." But the story begins before the dawn of time.

How can the scribes say that the Anointed One is the son of David? David said himself, by the power of the Holy Spirit, "The Lord said to my Lord, sit at my right hand, until I put your enemies beneath your feet." David himself calls him Lord — how then can he be his Son?

— Mark 12:35-37

Jesus is challenging the traditional teaching that the fulfillment of the messianic hopes will be merely a human ruler. The messiah is of an origin which causes even David awe. He may be of David's line — but he is much more than that.

My Father has worked before now, and I am working.

— John 5:17

I tell you, the Son can do nothing by himself, only what he sees the Father do. Whatever he does, the Son also does. The Father loves the Son, and reveals his actions to him. He will show him even greater things, so great that you will wonder at them. Just as the Father can raise the dead, giving them life, so the Son can give life to anyone he wishes. The Father does not judge any man, but has given all judgement to the Son, so that all will honor the Son just as they honor the Father. He who does not honor the Son does not honor the Father, who sent him.

What I tell you is true: he who hears me, and believes in him who sent me, has everlasting life and will not be condemned. He has passed from death to life.

What I tell you is true: the hour is coming, it is here right now, when the dead will hear the voice of the Son of God, and those who hear it will live.

As the father has life in himself, he has given the Son life in himself. He has also given him authority to judge, because he is the Son of Man.

Do not be surprised at this. The hour is coming when all who are in their graves will hear his voice. They will come out, if they have done good, and rise to life. Those who have done evil will rise to damnation.

I have no power to do anything. As I hear, I judge, and my

judgement is just, because I do not look for my own will but for the will of the Father who sent me.
— John 5:19-30

The Father himself, the one who sent me, has been my witness. You have never heard his voice, or seen him. You do not have his word living in you, because you do not believe the one he sent.

You search the scriptures, thinking that you will find eternal life there — and they testify to me. But you will not come to me, and have life. My honor does not come from men; but I know that you do not have the love of God at heart. I come in my Father's name and you will not receive me, though if someone were to come in his own name you would receive him. How can you believe — you who give honor to one another, but do not seek the honor which only God can give? Don't think I am the one who will accuse you to the Father; but there is one who will accuse you, and that is Moses, in whom you trust. If you really believed Moses you would believe me, because he wrote about me. If you do not believe his writings, how will you believe my words?
— John 5:37-47

My teaching is not mine, but comes from the one who sent me. If anyone is willing to do his will, that person will know the teaching, and whether it comes from God or merely comes from me. A person who teaches on his own authority looks out for his own glory; but the man who seeks the glory of the one who sent him is true: no falsehood is in him.

Isn't it true that Moses gave you the law — yet none of you keeps the law? Why do you try to kill me? I have done one work, and you are all upset. Moses gave you the command to circumcise (which came originally from the patriarchs), and you circumcise on the Sabbath. If circumcision takes place on the Sabbath day in fulfillment of Moses' law, why are you angry with me, for healing the whole of a man's body on the Sabbath? Do not pass judgement on the surface of things, but be sure that your judgement is just.
— John 7:16-24

You know me, and you know where I come from: I have not come on my own account. But he who sent me is true, and you do not know him. But I know him. I come from him, and he has sent me.
— John 7:28-29

It is true that I bear witness to myself. But my witness is true, because I know where I come from and where I am going. But you do not know where I come from or where I am going. You judge the way the world judges things, but I judge no man. If I did judge my judgement would be true, because I am not alone the judge, but I and he who sent me. It is written in your law that two witnesses are sufficient when testimony is taken. I bear witness to myself, and so does the Father, who sent me.
— John 8:14-18

You do not know me, or my Father. If you knew me, you would also know my Father.
— John 8:19

I go my way. You will look for me, but you will die in your sins. Where I am going you cannot come.
— John 8:21

The Gospel of John, as readers of the New Testament have always known, is quite different from Matthew, Mark, and Luke. In the three synoptic gospels Jesus' mission and its meaning are seen as unfolding slowly. His messianic role is not explicitly stated but is implied in Jesus' reaction to his disciples' answers to the question, "Who do men say that I am — and who do you say that I am?" It is revealed in other ways as well; but none of them are as direct as John is in asserting Jesus' messianic mission from the start. John assumes the faith of Christians in Jesus' messianic mission, and expounds the theology of Jesus' relationship to the Father. This is done during Jesus' discourse at the last supper, in which the disciples themselves are invited to share the relationship Jesus knows with his Father. It is also done in the above passages, where Jesus engages in angry dialogue with the leaders of the Jewish establishment. He accuses them of not attending sufficiently to the Spirit which breathes through the law and makes faith a living thing. They would recognize his divine authority if they were really living in the spirit of the patriarchs and prophets. While these accusations are directed in John's gospel against Jews, a fact which has been used by anit-Semites throughout the ages, this should not lead us to complacent Christian smugness. Precisely the same accusations can be made, and for precisely the same reasons, against any form of religion which waters down God's call to rules, regulations, and respectability. This was the force of Jesus' message. The religious establishment he encountered happened to be Jewish. Today's religious establishment happens to be Christian. The same charges apply to us now. What does it come down to, in the flesh? We all know priests and ministers who have turned beggars away (and laypeople too, of course); most of us have been relatively indifferent to suffering, especially the suffering close at hand. A reading of Matthew 25:31-46, and then a rereading of John in its light, might be in order. It is absolutely essential to recognize Christ — however he comes.

When you have lifted up the Son of Man, then you will know that I am he, and that what I do is not done on my own behalf; I speak the things my Father has taught me. He who sent me is with me: the Father has not left me alone, because I always do what pleases him.

— John 8:28-29

What I tell you is true: whoever commits sin is sin's servant. The servant does not always live in the house, but the Son lives there forever. Therefore, if the Son sets you free, you will truly be free.

I know that you are descendants of Abraham. But you want to kill me, because what I say offends you. I tell you what my Father has shown me, and you are doing what your father has shown you. If you were Abraham's children you would act as he did. But you want to kill me, a man who tells the truth he heard from God. Abraham would not do this. You do your father's work. If God were your father you would love me, because I come from God. I did not come on my own — he sent me.

Why can't you understand me? For the same reasons you do not accept my teaching. You belong to your father: the devil. You will act out his desires for him. He was a murderer from the start, and could not live with truth because there is no truth with him. When he tells a lie it is right at home, because he is a liar and the father of lies. Because I tell you the truth you do not believe me. Which of you can call me a sinner? And if I tell the truth, why won't you believe me? The person who is God's, hears God's words. Therefore you do not hear them — because you are not members of God's family.   — John 8:39-47

If I honor myself, that means nothing. My Father honors me, the one you call your God. But you do not know him. I do know him, and if I were to say, "I do not know him," I would be a liar, like you. But I

> know him, and live by his word. Your father Abraham waited joyfully for my day. He saw it and was glad.
> — John 8:54-56

> What I tell you is the truth: Before Abraham was, I am.
> — John 8:58

Jesus' identification of himself with the Father, his insistence that everything he does and says has its source in God, is underscored with this statement, perhaps the boldest and most shocking line in the New Testament. It is shocking because it is the highest blasphemy for a human being to claim divinity, and here Jesus uses of himself the name of God, "I Am," given to Moses from the burning bush. It was shocking enough that he should claim to be the Messiah, the Christ. But this is something new: never in messianic prophecy was it implied that the Messiah was divine. He would be divinely chosen, as David was, a king who would lead Israel to glory and unite all the peoples of the world in a just reign. The kingship Jesus identifies with is more staggering: it goes back beyond the creation of the world.

He reasserts this divine claim again when asked, "tell us plainly if you are the Christ."

> I told you, and you didn't believe me. The works I do in my Father's name testify to me. But you do not believe, because you are not numbered among my sheep, as I have said. My sheep hear my voice. I know them, and they follow me. I give them life, forever; they will never die, and no one can tear them out of my hand. My Father gave them to me; he is greater than all, and no man can tear them out of my Father's hands.
> My Father and I are one.
> — John 10:25-30

> Isn't it written in your law, "I said: you are Gods"? Scripture calls "gods" those to whom the word of God is delivered, and scripture cannot be ignored. So why do you say of the one consecrated and sent by the Father into the world, "You blaspheme," because I said "I am the Son of God"?
> If the works I do are not my Father's works, do not believe me. But if I do, believe the works themselves, even if you do not believe me, so that you may understand and come to believe that the Father is in me, and I am in him.
> — John 10:34-38

Unbelief was something Jesus encountered not only from his enemies but also from his own friends and family, though it was unbelief of a different kind. Jesus' brothers tell him to go directly to Jerusalem and force matters to a head by doing his "great works" there, if he can. They reproach him for not being more public; their words imply a lack of faith in his power, and a misunderstanding of his work. His answer shows his isolation, and a little weariness. Although he tells them that he will not join them in Jerusalem for the Feast of Tabernacles, he does go up later, but quietly; it is not time for a public confrontation. His answer to his brothers shows the distance which can exist even between Jesus and his followers.

My time has not come, not yet. Your time is always right. The world cannot hate you. But it hates me, for revealing how evil its ways are. Go up for the feast yourselves. I will not go up. My time has not come.
— John 7:6-8

Before his final journey to Jerusalem his followers expressed fears for Jesus' safety. They knew that he stood in danger of losing his life, and wondered why he dared to go to Jerusalem.

Doesn't daylight last for twelve hours? If a man walks during the day he doesn't stumble, because he has the light of this world to guide him. But if he walks at night, he stumbles, because he has no light.
— John 11:9-10

Two stories, linked by tradition, also connect Jesus' healing mission with his death. In Luke's account, a woman who may have been a prostitute (we are told that she was immoral) burst into a dinner at which Jesus was a guest, and kneeling at his feet, weeping, anointed him in great reverence and gratitude. In Matthew, Mark, and John (where her name is given as Mary) she is not called immoral, but anoints him; and the anointing is compared with the anointing of the dead. In Luke's version, Jesus' host is shocked at the action. Jesus says,

Simon, I have something to tell you. Once there was a creditor, who had two debtors. One owed him five hundred pieces of silver, the other fifty. But neither had any money, and he freely forgave both of them. Now tell me: which do you think would feel most love for him?

Of course it would be the one with the greatest debt. You see this woman? When I came into your house you did not provide me with water to wash my feet, but she has washed my feet with her tears, and wiped them with her hair. You did not kiss me, but from the time I came here she has not stopped kissing my feet. You did not anoint my head, but she has anointed my feet with ointment. So I tell you: her sins, which are many, are all forgiven because she has shown so much love. The person who is forgiven little loves little. — Luke 7:40-47

When there was some irritation expressed at the expense of the ointment, bought with money which might better have served the needs of the poor (a comment John gives to Judas, saying parenthetically that his concern was hypocritical), Jesus says that the anointing points to his death.

Leave her alone; why trouble her? She has done something good for me. The poor are always here, and you can help them any time you want to. But I am not always here with you. She has done the best she could, coming beforehand to anoint my body for burial. I tell you truthfully, wherever the Gospel is proclaimed in the world, what she has done will be proclaimed as her memorial. — Mark 14:6-9

You cannot follow me where I am going, not now; but you will follow me afterwards. — John 13:36

Jesus said these words (perhaps to Peter) to show two things. Now was his own time; Peter's had not yet come, nor had the time of death come for any of his followers. He had to die and rise, to show the way before them. Not only does this saying indicate the suffering which his first followers (and many of the later Christians) were to endure, but also the resurrection. We will all have to follow him in death; our hope is that even now, in life, we are following him into God's kingdom.

When he entered Jerusalem in triumph, knowing that this triumph would end in his death, Jesus was confronted with people who were shocked at children who greeted him with the cry, "Hosanna to the Son of David." Jesus answered the objection:

Haven't you read, "You have made your praise come from the mouths of children and babies at the breast?" — Matthew 21:16

The exuberance of the people who loved him was an echo of a joy which is as deep as the universe, a joy that the victory over evil was about to be accomplished. The vocal rejoicing of his disciples was a human echo of a joy which extended throughout all of creation.

> I tell you, if they kept quiet, the stones would immediately cry out.
> — Luke 19:40

THE SON OF MAN WILL BE BETRAYED: THE SUFFERING OF JESUS

Jesus was met throughout his life with the hostility of his enemies and the misunderstanding of his friends and family. Once, when many of his followers left him, he asked the twelve, "Will you also leave me?" Peter answered him as all Christians must: "Where else can we go? Your words are words of eternal life." (John 6)

There is loneliness in Jesus' question. His isolation seems to grow as he approaches the end of his life. And he warns his disciples that they must expect his death.

> You must always keep these words in your hearts: the Son of Man will be handed over into the power of men.
> — Luke 9:44

> Now we are going up to Jerusalem, where the Son of Man will be handed over to the chief priests and scribes, who will condemn him to death, and hand him over to the Gentiles. They will mock and beat him, spit on him and kill him. And on the third day he will rise.
> — Mark 10:33-34

This is an interesting counter to Christian anti-Semitism. Following his condemnation by the chief priests and scribes, the truly terrible thing happens: he is handed over to Gentiles.

When he spoke to his disciples of what lay in store for him, they tried to discourage such talk. Jesus may have been a wise, loving, and holy rabbi, but the disciples may have felt that his belief in his own violent death was an oddly morbid streak in an otherwise wholesome personality. Peter reproaches him: He should know, Peter says, that this must not happen to him. But Jesus answered,

Back, Satan. You are an obstacle to me, because you think as men think, not as God thinks. — Matthew 16:23

Jesus knew that his teaching would take him to the cross; he knew this in part because he knew how lethal the hatred of his enemies could be. He remembered the prophets, and John, who was "more than a prophet". He was warned by some Pharisees that he should stop his work and teaching and flee, because Herod planned to kill him. Jesus' reply was abrupt and harsh:

Go tell that fox, "Look: I will cast out devils and work cures today and tomorrow. On the third day I will be fulfilled." Still, I will travel today, tomorrow, and the day after, because it is impossible for a prophet to die away from Jerusalem.

O Jerusalem, Jerusalem, you have killed prophets and stoned those who were sent to you. How much I longed to gather your children together, the way a hen gathers her chicks beneath her wings, but you would not let me! Watch: your house is abandoned, and I tell you, you will not see me until the time when you say, "Blessed is he who comes in the name of the Lord." — Luke 13:32-35

THE BETRAYAL

I have chosen all twelve of you — but one is a devil.

— John 6:70

I tell you, one of my companions will betray me. It is one of the twelve, someone who shares the same dish. The Son of Man is going as he must, but how terrible it is for that man who betrays the Son of Man. It would be better for him if he had never been born.

— Mark 14:18-21

What I tell you is true — one of you will betray me. It is the one I will give this piece of bread, dipped into the dish.

That which you must do, do quickly.

— John 13:27

> Judas, do you betray the Son of Man with a kiss?
>
> — Luke 22:48

Judas' reasons for betraying Jesus have been variously explained. One common explanation is that he expected Jesus to be an earthly king, a political liberator, and in his disappointment he turned him over to the oppressors. Another is that he felt betrayal would actually force Jesus' hand and bring the Kingdom that much earlier. Another is that he was simply a scoundrel, and was predestined to act on Satan's behalf. The interior life of Judas is hidden from us even more than Jesus' — we are told at least that Jesus was "troubled". No doubt Judas' motives were complex and self-justifying; they ended in a dreadful remorse and suicide. This is some of Jesus' own sorrow as he approaches his death. "One of you who eats with me, who shares this dish, will betray me." "Do you betray the Son of Man with a kiss?" Even those who share the Lord's supper can be betrayers; those whose allegiance is outwardly for God but inwardly elsewhere betray him with a kiss. As in so much of scripture, the story continues in our own lives and the life of Jesus' church.

Judas was not the only one to abandon Jesus, though he alone betrayed him. Many originally sympathetic people had left him during his career. Now his followers began to feel a deep fear and confusion at the dark turn their lives with Jesus had taken. They believed that he came to usher in the kingdom of God, the messianic era in which the world would be reconciled into one peaceful and godly reality. On the brink of that moment their rabbi sat isolated, suddenly a stranger, dark. Their allegiance to him "because you have words of eternal life" must have been questioned deep in their hearts then. They accompanied him, nevertheless, to the garden of Gethsemane.

He told his friends to sit, while he went away to pray, accompanied by Peter, James, and John.

> My heart is so full of sorrow that I am nearly dead from it. Wait here, and stay awake.
>
> — Mark 14:34

> Abba — Father — for you everything is possible. Take this cup away from me. Yet not what I will, but what you will.
>
> — Mark 14:36

The time in Gethsemane is one of the most remarkable passages in the New Testament. Jesus confesses to his followers his own profound sorrow, and even asks for their help. This is unlike any other act of his in the gospels. His profound grief does not lead him away from obedience to the will of the Father, but it does lead him to ask for something different from what God seems, dreadfully, to have in mind for him. In Mark's gospel he calls the Father "Abba", a familiar word for father, much like our "papa". Then he went back to the disciples, perhaps feeling nothing, feeling that his prayer had gone into a void; he returned for human company and found his friends asleep.

You sleep? Couldn't you stay awake with me for even an hour? Be wakeful, and pray that you will not be tempted. The spirit is willing, but the flesh is weak. — Matthew 26:41

He returned to his prayer. When he went back to his friends a second time he found them still asleep. He left them, prayed a third time, and when he came back to them he said,

Sleep as much as you like now. Take your rest. The hour is here, when the Son of Man is betrayed to sinners. Get up. We must go. The one who betrays me is here. — Matthew 26:45-46

When Jesus was taken by those who had come to arrest him he told his captors to let his followers go their way:

I have told you that I am the one you are looking for. If you want me, let these men go. — John 18:8

I spoke openly, to everyone. I taught in the synagogue and the temple, where Jews always gather. I have said nothing secretly. So why do you ask me what I said? Ask those who heard me, ask what I told them: they know what I said. — John 18:20-21

Have you come with swords and clubs, as you would arm yourselves against a thief? When I was with you every day in the temple you made no move against me. But this is your hour, the time of darkness' power. — Luke 22:52-53

> Don't you believe that I could pray to my Father, and he would immediately send me more than twelve legions of angels? But then how would scripture be fulfilled?
>
> — Matthew 26:53-54

Following his prayer in Gethsemane, this statement that the Father would aid him with legions of angels, if only he asked for it, might look like an empty boast. He had asked simply not to be forced through this ordeal, and received no answer but the suffering which he underwent at the hands of his enemies and on the cross. There is something else here: it is a kind of irony, in one sense, because the help Jesus wanted (at one level, anyway) has been denied. But it is also a sign of an obedience which can go even to death, a surrender to a will which Jesus might not have understood completely, just as Abraham did not understand how God could demand the sacrifice of Isaac, through whom everything had been promised. There is no way for us to know Jesus' mind here, and it is impossible to know God's mind. But it may be that there was an alternative to his suffering, even now. Perhaps, if he were willing to withdraw from his own purpose on earth, he would have saved his life; if he were willing to allow scripture to go unfulfilled, he might have lived as the world usually defines life. He chose an obedience which was terrifying, and ended in a life we can only begin to imagine. Perhaps Jesus had been expecting a kingdom of God which would be a genuine restoration of David's glory, and found that God had other purposes, just as Abraham expected Isaac to father a holy nation, only to be asked for Isaac's death before the boy had a chance to father anyone. In both cases the gift God granted was greater than either may have expected.

It startles people to think that Jesus, being divine, was not omniscient at all times, and to think that he might have expected one thing and found another in its place is, to such people, blasphemy. But if Jesus was truly human, this would certainly have been part of his earthly life. And to think that it could not possibly be part of his divine calling, because of its humanity, is to make a separation between humanity and God which Jesus lived, and died, to overcome.

We know, at any rate, that Jesus believed all along in his mission to fulfill scripture, a belief which isolated him from his friends, who seemed always to misunderstand him; they misunderstood themselves as a consequence. Peter is often the spokesman for the twelve. As their representative he is the one who receives some of Jesus' hardest words, as well as some of his most tender ones. When Peter asks why he cannot follow Jesus to his destination (about which Peter is in the dark), he protests that he is so devoted that he would be willing to die for Jesus.

You will lay down your life for me? The truth is that the cock will not crow before you have denied me three times.
— John 13:38

And in the garden where he was captured Jesus tells Peter, who has attacked the attackers,

Put your sword away. Shouldn't I drink the cup which the Father has given me to drink?
— John 18:11

The suffering servant in Isaiah is known for his silence. When Jesus is taken before those who fear him, he is asked, "Are you the Christ? Are you the king of the Jews?" His answers turn the question back to them, in few words. Jesus, in the last pages of the gospels, is known not so much in his words, but in his silent acceptance. The words of Jesus thin out here to the most necessary words, which gain strength from the silence and suffering surrounding them. When asked if he was the Christ he answered,

If I say that I am, you will not believe me. If I ask you, you will not answer. But now you will see the Son of Man sitting at the right hand of God.
— Luke 22:67-69

Again and again in answer to the question, "Are you the Son of God?" he answers,

You say that I am.
—Mark 15:2, Matthew 27:11,
Luke 22:70, Luke 23:3

His answer is an accusation; his accusers want him to say something they can consider blasphemous. They are not actually looking for the truth. They want a victim. Rather than answer a too-simple "yes" or "no" to their questions, Jesus turns the question back. "You have said it . . . That is what you charge me with." He also asks,

> If what I have said is evil, then give real testimony to it. But if I have spoken well, why do you strike me?
> — John 18:23

They crucified him. The words which the gospels tell us he spoke during his final hours are few, but in a way they show the range of his concern — for his mother and the disciple he was closest to, John; for the man who, dying with him as a fellow-criminal, shows enough compassion to ask that Jesus be spared the taunts of another dying criminal; for those who have killed him; and finally these words show the submission of Jesus to the will of God, a submission which transcended even his sense of being abandoned.

> **Woman, here is your son.**
> **Here is your mother.**
> — John 19:26-27

> **Father, forgive them. They do not know what they are doing.**
> — Luke 23:34

> **I tell you, today you will be with me in paradise.**
> — Luke 23:43

> **I thirst.**
> — John 19:28

> **My God, my God, why have you forsaken me?**
> — Mark 15:34

> **It is ended.**
> — John 19:30

> **Father, I give myself into your hands.**
> — Luke 23:46

These words from the cross have been traditional Lenten meditations, particularly on Good Friday, words on which we are all asked to reflect. They are so stark, so unsatisfying. They are also strange, if we think of them as words spoken by a man, not by a phantom God-being impersonating a man (which is unfortunately the way too many of us see Jesus).

They are strange partly because it is uncomfortable for us to identify with a human being in such misery as Jesus was. It is much easier to deal with the notion that once upon a time there was a god who appeared to suffer to give us a proper sense of style, a way in which to suffer. It is so much worse to believe that he really suffered, that there was nothing more between him and despair than there would be between any suffering human being and despair. If anything, there was an even greater sense of abandonment. The distance between God and God, as Simone Weil wrote, is infinite; and she also wrote that Jesus' cry of abandonment was in itself enough to prove the divine origin of Christianity, since it is so true to the common human condition. (It is true that we might not feel so abandoned, personally. But those with the leisure to read this book, and the interest, are exempt from the hunger and fear which dominate most of the world. Our feeling of well-being is based on that exemption from the experience of most of our brothers and sisters, including those whose mental suffering and anxiety are not imaginable to those of us who feel smug at being unable to imagine the real extremes a mind can be taken to. The belief that Jesus' suffering included all of this, that it was taken on not by a disguised god, but by a loving human being, cannot be faced honestly without forcing us to re-evaluate our normal hard-heartedness.) It was at the depths of his suffering humanity that his complete obedience to the Father was revealed, and with it his divinity.

THE RESURRECTION

The crucifixion, resurrection, and ascension of Jesus should be seen as one continuous movement, the completion of a pattern which existed before time began and was revealed in Jesus. Paul writes in Philippians, "The divine nature was his from the first, but he did not hold on to his equality with God. He emptied himself, taking on the nature of a slave. In human likeness, revealed as a human being, he humbled himself, accepting even death in his obedience — death on a cross. Therefore God raised him to the heights and gave him a name higher than all other names, so that at Jesus' name every knee should bow, in heaven, on earth, and in the depths, and every tongue confess 'Jesus Christ is Lord', to God the Father's glory." The glory which the resurrection manifested is the heart of the good news: God has loved Jesus, and those who would be his friends, to this unimaginable extent. The gospels tell us that at several points Jesus alluded to his coming resurrection. "Destroy this temple, and in three days I will raise it up," he said (John 2:19), and the disciples believed he meant the temple in Jerusalem. Following his transfiguration on Mount Tabor, he told Peter, James, and John, "Do not tell anyone about what you have seen until the Son of Man rises from the dead." (Matthew 17:9) The night before his death he told his followers, "You will all lose faith, because it is written, 'I will strike down the shepherd and the sheep will scatter.' But when I have risen I will go before you into Galilee." (Mark 14:27-28) When asked by the high priest if he was the Christ, the anointed one, Jesus said, "The words are yours. But I tell you that after this you will see the Son of Man sitting on Power's right hand, coming on the clouds of heaven." (Matthew 26:63-64)

But his coming is more quiet. And one of the interesting things is that he first appears as a stranger. On the road to Emmaus, two of his followers do not recognize him, even as he talks to them in an effort to turn their discouragement to joy. They recognize him "in the breaking of the bread". When he asks Mary, "Why are you weeping?" she mistakes him for a gardener, until he says, very simply, "Mary". He calls her by name, and she recognizes him. Then he tells her,

>Do not cling to me, because I have not yet ascended to the Father. But go to my brothers, and say to them that I am going to ascend to my Father, and your Father, my God and your God.
>— John 20:17

>Thomas, put out your finger — here are my hands. Reach your hand into the wound in my side. Do not be faithless — believe. You believe me because you have seen me, Thomas. Blessed are those who have not seen me yet, but still believe.
>— John 20:27-29

>Do not be afraid. Go tell my brothers to go into Galilee, and they will see me there.
>— Matthew 28:10

What are you talking about as you walk along, that makes you so sad? How thick-headed, how slow you are to believe what the prophets said! Shouldn't the Messiah have suffered all these things, before coming into his glory? — Luke 24:17,25-26

Why are you troubled? Why are you brooding deep in your hearts? Look at my hands and feet — it is I. Touch me and see. A ghost does not have flesh and bones, as I do, and you can see that. Do you have anything here to eat?

Now you may see what I meant when I was with you, and said that everything Moses and the prophets and the psalmists wrote about must be fulfilled in me. — Luke 24:36-44

It was written that the Messiah had to suffer and rise from the dead on the third day, and that in his name repentance and forgiveness of sins should be preached everywhere, to all people, beginning with Jerusalem. You have seen all of this. Know this: I will send you what my Father has promised you. But wait here in Jerusalem until you are made strong with power from above. — Luke 24:46-49

Have you caught anything to eat, friends? You would find something if you cast your nets on the right side of the ship.

Now bring the fish which you have just caught.

Come and dine. — John 21:5-12

The occasions on which Jesus appeared as a stranger should teach us something which is echoed in Matthew 25: whatever we do to anyone is done to Christ, who comes to us as a stranger. Mary knows him when he calls her by her name, the disciples on the road to Emmaus know him in the breaking of the bread, and Peter and his companions in the boat see him first as a stranger; but when their nets are full to bursting with fish, and he invites them to dine, preparing the meal himself, "none of them dared ask, who are you?"

But Jesus told Mary, "I have not ascended to my Father." His work would be complete only when he had gone to the glory of his Father, continuing among us by the power of the Holy Spirit and the Spirit's power in his church. And so he addressed a question three times to Peter, and by the third repetition Peter must have remembered his denial of Jesus, also threefold.

Simon, son of John, do you love me more than you love anything else?

Then feed my lambs.
Simon, son of John, do you love me?
Then take care of my sheep.
Simon, son of John, do you love me?
Feed my sheep.

What I tell you is true: when you were young you fastened your belt and walked where you liked. But when you are old, you will stretch out your hands; another person will bind you and take you where you do not want to go.

Follow me.

— John 21:15-19

Simon protested his love for Jesus three times, and Jesus told him what the consequences of following him would be. Many members of the early church were called on to suffer the same kind of violence Jesus had suffered, a suffering which continues in many places today, in South Korea, parts of Latin America, the Philippines, the Soviet Union. The Body of Christ continues to suffer crucifixion. But in faith Christians know that they also are sustained by the power of the Holy Spirit, the power which raised Jesus from the dead. The resurrection is not something for another life — it begins now, and shows itself in the works of reconciliation. "You are mistaken in not knowing the scriptures, or God's power. When they have risen, people do not marry; they are like God's angels in heaven. But concerning the resurrection of the dead, haven't you read what God spoke to you, when he said, 'I am the God of Abraham, and the God of Isaac, and the God of Jacob?' God is not the God of the dead, but of the living." (Matthew 22:29-32)

When he rose to the Father, Jesus completed his mission, which continues in us, by the power of God's spirit.

Wait for what God has promised; you have heard me speak of it. John baptized with water, but not many days from now you will be baptized with the Holy Spirit.

— Acts 1:4-5

It is not for you to know the time or the hour when the Father will choose to act; that is in his hands. But you will receive power when the Holy Spirit comes to you, and you will be my witnesses in Jerusalem, in all of Judea, in Samaria, and in every part of the world.

— Acts 1:7-8

Tales of the Kingdom

Jesus spoke so often in stories and parables that when, during his last hours, he spoke plainly to his disciples they were surprised. Storytelling was an essential part of his teaching. Even in his most direct statements — those found in the sermon on the mount, for example — Jesus used comparisons and examples which were like the beginnings of fables: his followers were invited to "look at the lilies of the field . . . the birds of the air"; and those who followed his words were "like a man who built his house on solid rock," while those who failed to hear him were "like a man whose house was built on sand."

Why, it might be asked, didn't he speak to us more directly? We want to hear how we ought to behave, what we must do to be saved, and he tells a story. We want a blueprint, and we get a fable.

Stories and fables have throughout most of the world's history been a primary means of instructing people. It is our culture's peculiarity that they are thought to be more appropriate for the nursery than for adults. We have been led to believe that what we need to know is simple *information* — "just the facts, please" — and that everything beyond this is superfluous. (The word *poetry* has been debased because of this; you'll hear people say "there is more poetry than truth in that statement" — as if poetry were not perhaps the most concise way of speaking, as if it were an embellishment.)

But anyone literate knows that this is not true to our experience. Great works of fiction and poetry illuminate the depths of human experience as nothing else can. The psychiatrist Robert Coles has pointed out that even the greatest works of psychology fail to account for the human soul the way the writings of a novelist like Dostoevsky can.

This is because what we need to know in order to live cannot be reduced to simple facts or sets of instructions.

There is a width and a depth to a story which exists nowhere else, and this is especially true of Jesus' parables. The more a story like the story of the prodigal son (or, as it is more accurately called, the story of the merciful father) is considered, the more it reveals. And in trying to describe the kingdom of God, Jesus presents us with one image after another: it is like a seed, like leaven, like treasure; it grows, it is worth everything.

It was probably through his stories that Jesus became known to people. First there are the tales which give a sense of what the kingdom is about; then allegiance to him, his teaching, and his life. I have added relatively little comment here. A story says what it says, and says it so compactly that added words can detract and limit, rather than add to its meaning. There are only a few places where Jesus expands on the meaning of a parable. For the rest, the New Testament offers the parables straight, in the hope that they will resonate where they will in us.

Once a farmer went out to sow his fields. As he sowed, some seeds fell by the wayside, and birds came and ate them. Some fell on rocky ground, where there was not much soil. They grew right away, because the earth was shallow; when the sun was at its height they were scorched, and because they were rootless they withered away. Some fell among thorns, and the thorns grew around them and choked them. But others fell on good ground and brought forth fruit, some a hundredfold, some sixtyfold, some thirtyfold. Whoever can hear this, let him hear it.

It is given to you to know the mysteries of the kingdom of heaven, but it is not given to everyone. For whoever has, will be given more; whoever has not, will have even what little he has taken away.

So I speak to them in parables, because seeing, they do not see; hearing, they do not hear, or understand. In them Isaiah's prophecy is foretold: "Hearing you will hear, but not understand. Seeing you will see, and still not perceive, because the heart of this people has become coarse, their ears grown dull, their eyes they have closed, to keep them from seeing with their eyes, hearing with their ears, or understanding with their hearts, and from being converted and healed by me."

Your eyes are blessed, because they see, and so are your ears, because they hear. I tell you the truth: many prophets and many just men longed to see what you see, and did not see them; they longed to hear what you hear, and did not hear them.

So this is the parable of the sower: When anyone hears the word of the kingdom, but fails to understand it, the evil one comes, and seizes what was sown in his heart. This is the person whose seed fell by the wayside.

But the one who received the seed on rocky ground is the one who hears the word, and at first receives it joyfully. But he does not let it take root in him, it lasts only for awhile. When the word causes distress or persecution, he leaves it.

He who received the seed among thorns is the one who hears the word, but worldly concerns and wealth's allurements choke the word, and he does not bear its fruit.

The person who received the seed on good ground is the one who hears the word and understands it. It bears fruit — some a hundredfold, some sixtyfold, some thirtyfold. — Matthew 13:3-23

The kingdom of heaven is like a man who sowed his field with good seed. But while everyone was sleeping, his enemy came and sowed weeds where the wheat had been sowed, and crept away. When the wheat began to grow, the weeds also sprang up. So the man's servants came to him and said, "Master, isn't it true that you sowed good seed in your field? Why then are there weeds?" He told them, "An enemy has done this." Then the servants asked, "Should we pull up the weeds now?" "No," he answered. "You might uproot the wheat along with the weeds. Let them grow side by side until harvest time. At harvest I will tell the reapers, 'Gather up the weeds and tie them up for burning. But put all of the wheat in my barn.' " — Matthew 13:24-30

He who sows good seed is the Son of Man. The field is the world. The good seeds are the children of the kingdom, and the weeds are the children of the evil one. The enemy who sows them is the devil. The harvest is the end of the world. The reapers are the angels.

As the weeds are gathered and burned, so it will be at the end of the world.

The Son of Man will send his angels, and they will gather up from his kingdom everything offensive and all evil-doers, and throw them into a fiery furnace. Then there will be loud lamentation and the grinding of teeth. Then the just will shine like the sun in their Father's kingdom. Whoever can hear this, let him hear it. — Matthew 13:37-43

Pay attention to what you hear: because what you measure out will be measured out to you; and more as well. To the one who has, more will be given; from the one who does not have, even that little which he has will be taken.

This is what the kingdom of God is like: it is as if a man casts seed into the ground; he sleeps at night and rises during the day, while the seed sprouts and grows — how, he doesn't know, because the earth brings forth seed by itself, first the blade, then the single ear, then the whole corn plant.

But when the crop is full he puts his sickle to work, because harvest-time has come.

What is the kingdom of God like? What can we compare it to? It is like a mustard seed, which when it is planted is the smallest of all the seeds on earth. But when it has been planted it grows up to become greater than any other plant, putting out its great branches, large enough for the birds of the air to find shelter in its shadow.

— Mark 4:24-32

The kingdom of heaven is like yeast. A woman took it, mixed it with three measures of flour, and in the end the whole was leavened.

— Matthew 13:33

The kingdom of heaven is like a treasure hidden in a field. When a man finds it, he hides it again, and in joy he goes to sell everything he has, and buys the field. — Matthew 13:44

The kingdom of heaven is like a merchant who is always looking for valuable pearls. When he has found one worth more than any other, he goes, sells all he has, and buys it. — Matthew 13:45-46

The kingdom of heaven is like a net cast into the sea, which gathers in everything. When it was full it was drawn ashore; they sat down and gathered everything good and put it into vessels, but the bad was

thrown away. That is how it will be at the end of the world. The angels will come and divide the evil from the just, and cast them into a fiery furnace, where there will be loud lamentations and the grinding of teeth.
— Matthew 13:47-50

Have you understood all this? Therefore, every scribe who is able to understand the kingdom of heaven is like a wise householder, who is able to bring from his store of treasures both new and old things.
— Matthew 13:51-52

Once there was a man who had a great dinner, and invited many people to attend it. When the dinner was ready he sent his servant to the people who had been invited to tell them, "Come — everything is ready now."

One after another they made excuses. The first said to him, "I have bought some land and have to go look at it — please excuse my absence."

Another said, "I have just bought five yoke of oxen, and I must try them out — please excuse my absence."

Another said, "I have married a wife, so I am afraid I will not be able to attend."

The servant returned with the news, and the master of the house, angry now, said to his servant, "Quickly now, go out into the streets and alleys of the city, and bring to me the poor, the crippled, the lame, and the blind."

The servant said, "It has been done as you asked, lord, and there is room left over."

The lord said to the servant, "Go out to the highways and hedges, then, and make anyone you find there come in, to fill up my house. I tell you, none of the people I invited will taste my dinner."
— Luke 14:16-24

The kingdom of God overflows — it grows (like the mustard seed), it rises and enriches the whole (like the yeast). And God, the source and end of the kingdom, is the same way: he must be generous. We answer the generosity of God with paltry excuses, not seeing his generosity for what it is. But that generosity must be satisfied. Nothing will get in his way, or keep him from the wedding feast he longs to celebrate. We don't *have* to be guests; we have the freedom to be foolish and choose something other than to accept his gift, responding with gratitude to his graciousness.

The kingdom of heaven is like a king, who arranged a wedding feast for his son. But when he sent his servants out to gather the guests who were invited they would not come. So he sent other servants, and told them, "Say to the people who have been invited, I have prepared my dinner; the oxen and fattened cattle have been killed, and everything is ready for the feast. Come to the wedding."

But they took the news lightly and went about their ordinary business, one to his farm, another to his store, and others seized the servants, mistreated them, and then killed them.

The king was filled with rage when he heard this. He sent out his armies and destroyed the murderers, and their city was burned to the ground.

Then he said to his servants, "The wedding is ready. But because the people I invited proved themselves unworthy, go out to the highways, and invite anyone you find there to come to the wedding feast." So the servants went out to the highways and brought as many people as they could find into the feast, bad and good alike, and the wedding was filled with guests.

When the king came in to see the guests, he saw a man there who was not dressed for a wedding feast, and he said to him, "Friend, why is it that you came here without the right clothes for a wedding feast?" The man had nothing to say for himself. Then the king said to the servants, "Tie him, hand and foot, take him away and throw him into the darkness outside, where there will be weeping and the grinding of teeth."

Many are invited, but few are chosen.   — Matthew 22:2-14

There was once a man who planted a vineyard. He left it in charge of some farmers, and went on a voyage to a far-away land. He was gone for a long time, but when the season was at hand he sent a servant to the farmers, to tell them that they should give him the vineyard's yield. The farmers beat the servant, and sent him away empty-handed.

He sent another servant. They beat him too, treated him shamefully, and sent him away with nothing.

He sent a third. They wounded him and threw him out.

Then the lord of the vineyard said, "What will I do now? I will send my son, the one I love so much. Perhaps they will be reverent to him, when they see him."

But when the farmers saw him they thought to themselves, "This is the heir. Let's kill him, so that the inheritance will pass to us." So they threw him out of the vineyard and killed him.

Now what will the lord of the vineyard do? He will come and destroy the farmers, and give the vineyard to others.   — Luke 20:9-16

Do not forgive your brother seven times — forgive him seventy times seven.

There was a king once, who wanted to look into the accounts of his servants. When he began to check them a man was brought to him who owed ten thousand talents, but, because he could not pay, his lord gave orders for him to be sold, along with his wife and children and all his belongings, to meet the payment.

The servant fell in reverence before his feet and said, "Lord, please be patient with me: I will pay everything I owe." And the servant's lord was moved with compassion. He let him go, and forgave him everything he owed.

But that servant went out and when he met one of his fellow servants, who happened to owe him only 100 denarii, he grabbed him, choked him, and said, "Pay me what you owe!" When the other servant fell at his feet, asking, "Have patience! I will pay everything!" he would not listen. Instead, he had him jailed until he paid his debt.

When the other servants saw what had happened they were grieved, and went to their lord to tell him everything that had happened. The lord called the servant to him and said, "You wicked servant! I forgave you everything you owed, because you begged me to. Shouldn't you have been compassionate towards your fellow servant, just as I was compassionate with you?"

His lord was extremely angry. He handed the servant over to torturers, until he paid everything he owed.

And this is what my heavenly Father will do to you, if you do not forgive everyone from the bottom of your hearts.   — Matthew 18:21-35

There was once a rich man who had a steward, and he heard accusations that the steward had been wasting his property. So he called him and said, "What is this I hear of you? Hand over your accounts; you can no longer be my steward."

The steward said to himself, "What will I do now? My lord has taken away my stewardship, but I am unable to dig for a living, and I am ashamed to beg. I know what I must do: I must do something which will make others welcome me when I have been made to leave my job." So he called in everyone who was in debt to his master. He said to the first, "How much do you owe my lord?" "One hundred measures of oil," he answered. The steward said, "Quickly, take your bill, sit down, and write fifty." He said to another, "How much do you owe?" "One hundred measures of wheat," he answered. "Take your bill, then," the steward said, "and write eighty."

The master praised the unjust steward for his shrewdness; because the children of this world behave more wisely in dealing with one another than the children of light.

I tell you, use your defiled money to win yourself friends, so that when it fails you they will receive you into eternal dwelling places.

The one who is faithful is small matters will be faithful in great matters; the one who is unjust in small matters will be unjust in great matters. If you cannot even be trusted with money, defiled as it is, who will trust you with what is truly valuable? If you have not been trustworthy with something which belongs to another, who will give you that which belongs to you alone?

No servant can serve two masters. Either he will hate one and love the other, or he will be faithful to one, and betray the other. You cannot serve God and money.
— Luke 16:1-13

This is one of the most puzzling parables. Jesus commends the unjust steward for his shrewdness. It may be because this man, unjust as he was, had been careful enough to think ahead, and knew what to do in a time of crisis, a time he was prepared for. If someone who is unjust is capable of such shrewdness, shouldn't the children of God be even more alert? The earthly goods with which the steward dealt are small matters, compared to the larger matter of God's kingdom. Jesus makes it clear that he is not recommending a worldly attitude. When he says that no man can serve both God and money he is not simply moralizing; he does not say that no man should do so . . . it is impossible to do so. If you try to serve God and money, what you call "God" will in fact be an idol, a God cut down to fit our desires, and not the God of the living, the God who demands wholehearted allegiance.

There was a man who had two sons. The younger son said to his father, "Father, give me the part of the inheritance I will receive." So the father divided his estate between them. Shortly thereafter the younger son took everything he had and traveled to a far away country, where he squandered it all away on stupid things.

When he had spent everything he had, a terrible famine struck the country. The son found himself poor. So he went to work for someone in that country, who sent him into the fields to feed the pigs.

He would have eaten the husks which were given to pigs gladly, he was so hungry, but no one gave him anything. When he came to his senses the younger son said, "My father's hired servants have more than enough bread to eat — and here I am, dying of hunger! I will get up and go to my father, and tell him, 'Father, I have sinned against heaven and you. I am not worthy to be called your son. Give me only the place of a hired hand.'"

He got up, and returned to his father. But when he was still at some distance, his father saw him. Moved with compassion, he ran towards his son, threw his arms around his neck and kissed him.

The son said to him, "Father, I have sinned against heaven and against you. I am not worthy to be called your son." But the father told the servants, "Get the best robe and put it on him. Put a ring on his hand, and shoes on his feet. Bring out the fattest calf, kill it, and we will feast happily. My son was dead — now he is alive again! He was lost, and now he has been found." They began to rejoice.

The older son had been working in the field. As he returned to the house he heard the sounds of festivity. Calling one of the servants, he asked what it all meant. "Your brother has come," the man said. "Your father has killed the fatted calf, because he has had his son restored safe and sound."

He was angry and would not go in. So his father came out to him, pleading with him. But he answered his father, "Look at all the years I served you. At no time did I disobey you. But you never gave me even a baby goat, to feast with my friends. Now your son has returned — the one who wasted all your money on prostitutes — and as soon as he comes in you kill the fatted calf."

"Son," his father said, "You are always with me, and everything I have is yours. But it was right for us to feast and rejoice, because your brother was dead, and lives again. He was lost, and is now found."

— Luke 15:11-32

The younger son in asking for his inheritance is really asking for his father to die; that is when inheritances are given. His father, nevertheless, allows him this freedom. When the son comes to his senses, realizing (if only for the most base reason — his hungry stomach) that he has acted wrongly, he returns home contrite. The father does not even wait for him to get to the door — he has been watching for him, and runs toward him to embrace him joyfully. This parable of God's merciful, patient love is one of the most moving passages in scripture. But it is easy to sympathize with the older son, who was obedient all his life. His father's words, consoling him, reveal one of the secrets of the kingdom: it exists to reconcile all things, and to celebrate that reconciliation.

WHO IS MY NEIGHBOR?

Once there was a man who went down from Jerusalem to Jericho. Thieves attacked him on the way; they stripped him of his clothing, wounded him, and left him half dead.

It happened that a priest passed that way. When he saw the victim he passed him by, on the other side of the road.

Then a Levite came along, and did the same thing: when he saw the man, he passed by on the other side.

But a Samaritan traveling that way came to the place where the man lay. When he saw him he was touched with compassion and went over to him. He cleaned his wounds with oil and wine, put him on his own beast, and brought him to an inn. There he took care of him. When he departed on the following day he paid the innkeeper and told him, "Take care of him. If you have to spend any more on him, do so and I will repay you when I return."

Which of these three do you think was the true neighbor to the man who fell among thieves?

The one who showed mercy.

Go, and do the same.

— Luke 10:30-37

The fields of a rich man once yielded a great harvest. So he thought to himself: "What shall I do? I have no room for all of my crops." Then he thought: "This is what I will do: I will pull down the barns I have, and build larger ones. There I will put all of my crops and everything I own. And I will say to my soul, 'Soul, you have everything you need laid up for years — take it easy, eat, drink, be merry!' "

But God said to him: "You fool! Tonight your soul will be demanded of you. Then who will own all of those things you have gathered?"

This is the way it is with the person who lays up treasure for himself, but is not at all rich as far as God is concerned.

— Luke 12:16-21

Which one of you, if he has a hundred sheep, will not leave ninety-nine in the wilderness and go after one which is lost, and search until he finds it? When he has found it he puts it across his shoulders and rejoices. And when he comes home he calls his friends and neighbors together, saying, "Rejoice with me! I have found my sheep, the one I lost!" I tell you that this is like the joy in heaven over one sinner who repents — more than the joy shown over ninety-nine who do not need to repent.

In the same way, what woman who has money and loses a silver piece will not light a candle and sweep the house, looking everywhere until she finds it? When she finds it, doesn't she call her friends and neighbors in, saying, "Rejoice with me! I have found the silver piece I lost!" In the same way, I tell you, the angels rejoice in God's presence over one repentant sinner.

— Luke 15:4-10

This is another example of God's unlimited love, a love which is quite absurd in human terms. "Which one of you would not leave a flock of sheep alone to look for one? No shepherd in his right mind would. Nor would anyone sweep out a whole house, looking for a tiny coin. But this is God's attitude toward the sinner: he is that much in love with us.

Two men went to the temple to pray. One was a Pharisee. The other a tax collector.

The Pharisee stood forward, and prayed this way: "I thank you, God, that I am not like other people — extortioners, unfair, adulterous;

like this tax collector, for example. I fast twice every week, and give away a percentage of what I own."

The tax collector stood far away. He did not even dare to lift up his eyes, but struck his breast over and over again, saying, "God, have mercy on me, a sinner."

I tell you, this man went home justified rather than the other. Everyone who holds himself up will be thrown down. The one who is truly humble will be lifted up. — Luke 18:10-14

This parable recommends the proper attitude toward prayer — that is to say, it tells us how we should always stand before God: knowing our sinfulness and our need for his help. It is also a story which gets you coming and going. Where do you put yourself in this story? Are you the tax collector praised by Jesus for his honesty? Do you compare yourself favorably when you look at yourself next to the Pharisee? Then you are being the way he was, thanking God that you are not like other people, like all those terrible Pharisees. There is no room in the kingdom for religious self-satisfaction or smugness.

Who is the faithful, wise servant, the one the lord will appoint ruler of the house, to give everyone his portion of food at the right time? Blessed is the servant whom the lord finds working this way when he comes. I tell you truthfully, he will make him ruler over everything he owns!

But if the servant says in his heart, "My lord will not return for a long time," and begins to beat the men and women who work for him, and becomes a glutton and a drunkard, then the servant's lord will come when he is not expected. He will come at an unknown time, and cut him to bits, and the servant will be no better than those without faith.

The servant who knew what his lord wanted, but did not prepare himself or obey, will be given a terrible flogging. But the one who was not aware of the lord's will, even though he is guilty of things which deserve a flogging, will be flogged less severely.

This is because much is demanded of the one who has been given much; if people have trusted someone with many things, they will ask more of him. — Luke 12:42-48

The kingdom of heaven is like a man who traveled to a far away land. He called his servants together, and put them in charge of what he owned. He gave one five talents, another received two, another got one. He gave each one the amount he was able to handle, and left on his journey.

Then the one who had received five talents took them and invested them, earning another five. The same thing was done by the man with two talents, and he earned another two.

But the man who had received one talent dug a hole in the ground and buried his lord's money.

After a long time the lord returned to his servants, and asked them what they had done with his money.

The one who had received five talents came forward with the additional five. "Lord," he said, "you gave me five talents. Look: I have used them to earn five more talents." His lord answered him, "Well done, good and faithful servant! You have been faithful over a few things — now I will make you ruler over many things. Enter into the joy of your lord!"

The one who had received two talents also came forward and said, "See, lord, you left me with two talents — and I have earned two more!" "Well done, good and faithful servant!" the lord said. "Because you have been faithful over a few things, I will make you ruler over many things. Enter into the joy of your lord!"

Then the one who had received one talent came forward and said, "Lord, I know that you are a hard man. You reap what you have not planted, and gather where you have not scattered. So I was afraid. I buried your talent in the ground. Here it is: now you have back what is yours."

The lord answered him, "You wicked, lazy servant! You knew that I reap where I have not planted, and gather where I have not scattered. You should have deposited my money, so that on my return I could receive back what I own, with added interest. Take the talent from him, and give it to the man who has ten talents. The one who has will be given more, until he has an abundance. But the one who has not will lose what he has. Throw the unprofitable servant into the outer darkness, where there is weeping and the grinding of teeth."

— Matthew 25:14-30

There was a man who had a fig tree planted in his vineyard. He came to it and looked for fruit, and found none.

He said to the vine dresser, "For three years now I have come to this fig tree looking for fruit, and I have not found any! Cut it down — why waste the ground on it?"

The vine dresser answered him: "Lord, leave it alone this one last year. I will dig around it, and manure it. Then if it bears fruit, good. If after all that it does not, then cut it down." — Luke 13:6-9

The kingdom of heaven is like a householder, who went out early in the morning to hire workers for his vineyard. When he and his workers had agreed on a wage — one denarius per day — he sent them into the vineyard.

He went out again at the third hour and saw others standing around the market place with nothing to do, so he said to them, "Go into the vineyard with the others, and I will pay you the right wage." And they did so.

He went out again, at the sixth and ninth hour, and did the same.

At the eleventh hour he went out again, and found others standing idle. He said to them, "Why be idle all day?" They answered, "No one has hired us." He told them, "Go into the vineyard with the others."

When evening came, the lord of the vineyard told his steward, "Call the laborers and give them their wages, starting with the last and ending with the first."

When the ones who were hired at the eleventh hour came forward they each received a denarius. When the first came forward they assumed that they would receive more, but they also received one denarius each. And when they received it they complained to the master of the house, saying, "The last men hired worked only for an hour, but you have put them on a par with us, who were burdened with a whole day's heat and work."

He answered one of them. "Friend," he said, "I haven't wronged you. Didn't you agree to work for a denarius? Take what is yours, and go. I wish to pay the last what I paid you. Isn't it my right to do what I wish to do with what I own? Why see something evil in the fact that I choose to be kind?"

In this way, the last will be first, and the first, last.

— Matthew 20:1-16

There was once a judge who lived in a city. He had no fear of God, or respect for human beings.

There was also a widow who lived in that city. Again and again she came to the judge saying, "Give me a verdict against my adversary."

At first he would not. But after awhile he said to himself, "Although I am not afraid of God and have no respect for human beings, I will give the verdict she asks for; otherwise she will continue to bother me with her complaints."

Hear what the unjust judge says! Will not God give justice to those he has chosen, when they cry day and night to him, even when he waits a long time to help them? He will render his justice speedily, I tell you.

But when the Son of Man comes, will he find faith on earth?

— Luke 18:2-8

In the sermon on the mount Jesus says that if we would give our own children wholesome food, "evil as we are," won't a loving God give us even greater things? He uses the same method here, in a story which was told, Luke says, to encourage his followers to pray always, and not to be discouraged.

You should know that if the householder knew at what time the thief was coming, he would keep watch; he would not let his house be ransacked. So you should be watchful: the Son of Man will come when you are not expecting it.

Who is the faithful and wise servant, the one his lord sets over the household, to give everyone the right portion of food at the proper time? Blessed is the servant who is found at work, when his lord comes. I tell you truthfully, he will make him ruler over everything he owns.

But if the servant is evil, and says in his heart, "My lord is delayed," and begins to beat the other servants and eat and drink with drunkards, his lord will arrive on a day when he is not looked for, at an unexpected hour; he will slaughter him, and he will end where the hypocrites are, where there is weeping and the grinding of teeth.

— Matthew 24:43-51

The kingdom of heaven is like ten bridesmaids who took their lamps and went to meet the bridegroom. Five were wise and five were foolish.

The foolish ones took their lamps, but took no oil with them. The wise took vessels of oil with them, along with their lamps. They rested as they waited for the bridegroom, who was late.

Then at midnight a shout went up: "The bridegroom has come! Go out to meet him!" And all the virgins got up and trimmed their lamps.

The foolish bridesmaids said to the wise, "Give us some of your oil — our lamps have gone out." The wise answered, "We will not — there isn't enough for all of us. Go out to the store and buy some for yourselves."

While they were out on their errand the bridegroom came. Those who were ready went in with him to the wedding, and the door was shut. Then the other bridesmaids arrived, and called "Lord, Lord, open the door for us." But he answered them, "Truly, I do not know you."

Keep watch, then; because you do not know the day or the hour when the Son of Man will come.   — Matthew 25:1-13

Strive to come through the narrow door; many will try to enter, I tell you, and they will not be able.

Once the master of the house has arisen and shut the door, and you stand outside knocking, calling, "Lord, Lord, open to us," he will answer you: "I do not know where you come from." Then you will begin to say, "We have shared meals with you, and you taught in our streets." But he will say, "I tell you, I do not know where you come from. Leave me, all of you who are wicked."

There will be weeping and the grinding of teeth, when you see Abraham, Isaac, and Jacob, and all of the prophets in the kingdom of God, and you yourselves thrown out.

People will come from the east, the west, the north, and the south, and will sit down to the feast in the kingdom of God. Some who are last will be the first then, and some who are first will be last.

— Luke 13:24-30

The narrow gate is the way of wholehearted devotion to God and his kingdom. We cannot, as Jesus stresses in other places, have a divided allegiance to God. This wholeheartedness is critical: it is quite literally a matter of life and death. But rather than fear a fiery hell, we should see the metaphors Jesus used to tell us of the kingdom: it is a feast, to which we are invited. Hell begins not with God but in our hearts, in our resistance to the gift God offers.

Once there was a rich man. He dressed in purple and fine linen, and feasted lavishly every day.

There was also a beggar named Lazarus. Covered with sores he lay at the rich man's gate, longing for the crumbs which fell from the table. Dogs licked at his sores.

Finally the beggar died. He was carried into the arms of Abraham by angels. The rich man died as well, and was buried.

He lifted up his eyes in hell, tormented, and saw Abraham far away, with Lazarus in his arms. He cried out and said, "Father Abraham, have mercy on me. Send Lazarus; have him dip his finger in water to cool my tongue for me. I am in agony in this fire."

But Abraham said, "Son, remember that during your lifetime you had good things. Lazarus at the same time suffered evil. But now he is comforted, and you are tormented. Besides, there is a great gulf, which has been placed between us, and those who would go from here to there cannot; nor can anyone come here from there."

Then the man said, "I beg you, Father, send him to my father's house, to tell these things to my five brothers and keep them from coming to this place of torment." Abraham answered, "They have Moses and the prophets — let them hear them."

He said, "No, Father Abraham — but if one comes to them from the dead they will repent."

Abraham answered, "If they do not hear Moses and the prophets, they will not be persuaded even if someone rises from the dead."

— Luke 16:19-31

When the Son of Man comes in his glory, and all the holy angels with him, he will sit on his glorious throne, and all the peoples of the world will be gathered before him.

He will separate them, one from another, as a shepherd divides his sheep from his goats. He will place the sheep at his right hand, the goats at his left.

Then the King will say to those on the right hand, "Come, my Father has blessed you. Inherit the kingdom which has been ready for you from the day of the world's creation. I was hungry, and you fed me. I was thirsty, and you gave me drink. I was a stranger, and you took me in. When I was naked, you clothed me; you visited me when I was sick, and came to see me in prison." Then the righteous will ask, "Lord, when did we see you hungry, and feed you? Or thirsty, and give you a drink? When did we take you in, as a stranger, or clothe you when you were naked? When did we see you sick, or in prison, and visit you?" The King will answer, "I tell you truthfully, whenever you have done it to the least one of my brothers, you have done it to me."

Then he will say to those at his left hand: "Leave me, you accused ones, and go into the fire which lasts forever and was prepared for the devil and his angels. I was hungry, and you gave me no food; I was thirsty, and you gave me nothing to drink; I was a stranger, and you did not take me in; naked, and you did not clothe me; sick, and in prison, and you did not visit me." Then they will also ask, "Lord, when did we see you hungry, or thirsty, or a stranger, or naked, or sick, or in prison, and did not help you?" He will answer them, "I tell you truthfully, whenever you did not do it to the least of my brothers, you did not do it to me." And they will go away into a punishment which lasts forever; but those who are righteous will have eternal life. — Matthew 25:31-46

People who criticize the "social gospel" are right to say that Jesus was not primarily concerned with political liberation. But this passage, and the story of Lazarus, shows that Christians not only cannot ignore the plight of the suffering — it tells what will happen if they do.

I tell you truthfully, he who does not enter the gate of the sheepfold, but climbs in some other way, is a thief, a robber. But he who enters the gate is the shepherd of the sheep. The gatekeeper opens the gate for him, and the sheep hear his voice. He calls his sheep by name, and leads them out. When he has brought his sheep out he goes before them, and the sheep follow him, because they know his voice. They will not follow a stranger, but will run away from him, because they do not know the voice of strangers.

Truly, I am the gate of the sheepfold. All who come before me are thieves and robbers, but the sheep did not hear them. I am the gate. Anyone who enters through me will be saved, and he will go in and out, and find pasture. The thief comes for nothing but theft, murder, and destruction. I have come so that they might have life, and have it in abundance.

I am the good shepherd. The good shepherd lays down his life for the sheep. But the hired hand, who is not a shepherd, who does not own the sheep, leaves the sheep and runs away when he sees the wolf coming, and the wolf catches the sheep and scatters them. The hired hand runs away because he is hired, and does not care about the sheep.

I am the good shepherd. I know my sheep and they know me. As the Father knows me, so I know the Father; and I lay down my life for the sheep. I have other sheep who are not of this fold. I must lead them too. They will hear my voice, and there will be one fold and one shepherd.

This is why my Father loves me: because I lay down my life, to take it up again.

No man takes it from me: I lay it down myself. I have the power to lay it down, and power to take it up again. I have received this commandment from my Father. — John 10:1-5,7-18

The Heart of the Teaching

It takes a certain nerve to take any of Jesus' words away from the rest, and call them the heart of his message. Of course everything Jesus said and did must be considered vital to an understanding of his teaching. Here I have tried to gather those of his sayings which speak directly of what we are to believe, and become. His teaching continues in his instructions to his disciples, his hard sayings, his tales and parables; this section deals with his most direct statements of belief. Not that his other sayings are "embroidery" — they are also essential — but passages like Matthew, chapters five through seven, and the discourse of Jesus at the last supper, as recorded in John's gospel, reveal in a condensed form the difference between Christianity's claim and that of other religions, something which is especially clear in John. We are meant to share God's life; but this is not something we can claim, or have a right to. It is a completely unearned gift. As long as we have enough ego left to try to claim it on our own, we will be unable to accept or receive it. We must empty ourselves to make room for the coming of God. That emptying is something Matthew's account of the sermon on the mount emphasizes. Matthew's sermon on the mount is in a sense continuous with all of Jewish tradition. John's account of the last supper gives us the specifically Christian vocation. We are to love as God loves. But how can we love as God loves, or create the space which God can fill with God's own life, until we find the singlemindedness of the sermon on the mount? It is one thing to know, as a cold doctrine, that God, revealed in Christ, is the vine, and we are the branches. It is another to know where the vine ends and the branch begins; it requires the discipline and attention which Matthew teaches, and the ecstatic hope which John celebrates.

The time is here; the Kingdom of God is at hand. Repent, and believe the good news.
— Mark 1:15

Those who are healthy do not need a doctor, but those who are sick do. I have not come to call the righteous to repent, but sinners.
— Mark 2:17

The first of all the commandments is, "Hear, O Israel! The Lord our God is one. And you must love the Lord, your God, with all your heart, all your soul, all your mind, and all your strength." This is the first commandment. And the second is like it; it is this: "You must love your neighbor as yourself." There are no commandments greater than these.
— Mark 12:29-31

On these two commandments the whole of the law and the prophets are built.
— Matthew 22:40

Until John came, there were the law and the prophets. But since then the Kingdom of God has been preached, and everyone forces his way in. Heaven and earth will pass away more easily than any dot, any line, in the law.
— Luke 16:15-18

Who is my mother? Who are my brothers? Whoever does the will of my Father in heaven is my brother, and sister, and mother.
— Matthew 12:48-50

There is no man who has left his house, his brothers, sisters, father, mother, wife, children, or land for my sake and the sake of the good news who will not be rewarded one hundred times as much in this age — houses, brothers, sisters, mothers, children, land — and persecutions as well; and in the world to come he will have eternal life. But many who are first will be last, and the last first.
— Mark 10:29-31

What I tell you is true: unless you turn around and become like little children you will not enter the Kingdom of Heaven. Whoever humbles himself, like this child, is greatest in the Kingdom of Heaven. And whoever receives a child like this in my name receives me. But if a

man is a cause of scandal to one of these little ones who believe in me, it would be better for him if a rock were tied to his neck and he drowned in the depths of the sea. How it will be for the world, because of these offenses! It is true that they must come, but how hard it is for that man who causes the offense!
— Matthew 18:3-7

Make sure that you do not despise one of these little ones. I tell you, their angels in heaven continually see the face of my Father, who is in heaven.
— Matthew 18:10

The statement that we must become like children is one which has been variously interpreted: one common interpretation is that we must trust in God as children trust in their parents. Another is that we must shed the defenses we learn as adults, all the phony worldliness, and learn to be simple again. But as true as these recommendations may be, it should be remembered that our modern regard for children, and the attention we pay to the different ways they think and act, are modern phenomena. It is true that Jesus recommends the wholeheartedness and simplicity of children, and when he refers to "these little ones who believe in me" he means his simple followers, the ones who are as wholehearted as a disciple should be. But there is something else here as well: a child has no rights, but is completely dependent on his father and mother. It is this self-emptying, and total dependence on God, which are stressed here as well.

Whoever receives you receives me, and to receive me is to receive the one who sent me. Whoever receives a prophet as a prophet should be received, will receive a prophet's reward. And whoever receives a good man as a good man should be received, will receive the reward due a good man. And whoever gives one of these little ones even a cup of cold water because he is a follower of mine, he will certainly not be left without a reward.
— Matthew 10:40-42

THE SERMON ON THE MOUNT

The sermon on the mount, as presented by Matthew, stresses that Jesus was a true son of the covenant, a Jew whose loyalty to the law led him to oppose what he saw as a stale and legalistic allegiance on the part of the leaders of the Jewish community. What has been overlooked too often is the fact that the sermon on the mount is a summary of what was best in Pharasaical Judaism. (Jesus' defense of the doctrine of the resurrection which awaits mankind at the end of time is also Pharasaical.) It is a shock to some people to learn that Jesus' "love your neighbor as yourself" is exactly what he said it is: the law and the prophets. It can be found in the Old Testament, and adds nothing new. The most Christian of all prayers, the "Lord's prayer", is a summary of the first six of the eighteen benedictions found in the Hebrew prayer book. Even the most radical part of the sermon on the mount — the paradoxes found in the beatitudes — are statements which echo the hope of the prophets, as Mary's song of praise also does: the mighty are thrown down, the weak and humble are raised up.

Blessed are those who know how poor they are. The kingdom of heaven is theirs.

Blessed are those who are sorrowful: they shall be comforted.

Blessed are the gentle: the earth will be theirs.

Blessed are those who hunger and thirst after justice. They will be satisfied.

Blessed are the merciful. Mercy will be shown to them.

Blessed are the pure in heart. They will see God.

Blessed are the peacemakers. They will be called God's children.

Blessed are those who suffer because they do right. Theirs is the Kingdom of Heaven.

You are blessed when people scorn and persecute you, and speak evil against you, because you are followers of mine. Rejoice, be glad. Your reward in heaven is great, because they treated the prophets in exactly the same way.

You are the salt of the earth. But if the salt loses its flavor, how good is it? It is good for nothing and is thrown away to be trampled by everyone.

You are the light of the world. A city built on a hill cannot be hidden.

People don't light candles and then hide them under baskets; instead, they put them in candlesticks, to light the whole house.

Let your light shine before everyone, so that when people see your good works they will give glory to your Father in heaven.

Do not think that I came to destroy the law and the teaching of the prophets. I did not come to destroy — I came to fulfill.

I tell you that this is true: until heaven and earth pass away, not the smallest portion of the law may be set aside, not until everything has been fulfilled.

For this reason, whoever breaks the least commandment and teaches others to do so will be the least in the kingdom of heaven. But whoever keeps the commandments and teaches others to do so will be great in the kingdom of heaven.

I tell you, you must be better than the scribes and Pharisees; otherwise you will never be able to enter the kingdom of heaven.

You have heard how they said in the old days, "You shall not kill; whoever kills may be judged for it." But I tell you this: whoever is angry with his brother can be judged for it; whoever derides his brother may be taken to court; whoever calls his brother a fool will pay for it in hell's fire.

If, while you are on your way to the altar, you remember that your brother has something against you, stop and leave your gift; go and be reconciled with your brother, and then you will be able to offer your gift.

Come to terms with your opponent as soon as you can. Otherwise you may be handed from the judge to the officer and from the officer to jail. I tell you, you will not be released until you have paid the full fine.

In the old days they said, "You shall not commit adultery." But I tell you, whoever looks lustfully at a woman has already committed adultery in his heart. If your right eye is a problem, tear it out and throw it away. It is better for you to lose one part of your body than to be thrown, the whole of you, into hell. If your hand causes you problems, cut it off and throw it away. Better to lose a hand than to lose yourself in hell.

It was said, "Whoever wishes to divorce his wife can give her notice of divorce." But I say, whoever puts his wife away from himself (except in the case of adultery) causes her to commit adultery. And whoever marries a divorced woman commits adultery.

Again, it was said in the old days, "Do not break the oaths you have made. You shall do what you have sworn before the Lord." But I tell you, do not swear oaths at all — not in the name of heaven, because that is God's throne, nor by earth, for that is his footrest, nor by Jerusalem, for that is the city of the King. Do not even swear by your own head — you don't have the power to make one hair white or black! Instead, let your language be "yes", when you mean yes, "no", when you mean no. Anything else comes from evil.

You have heard the saying, "An eye for an eye and a tooth for a tooth." But I tell you, do not oppose the evildoer. If someone strikes your right cheek, offer him the left. If anyone sues you for your coat, give him your cloak as well. And whoever forces you to walk a mile with him, go another mile with him. Give to the one who asks; do not turn away from a borrower.

You have heard it said that you should love your neighbor and hate your enemy. But I tell you, love your enemies, bless those who curse you, pray for those who treat you with scorn and persecute you. In this way you will be children of your Father in heaven. He makes his sun rise on the evil and the good alike, and sends rain to fall on both the just and the unjust.

If you love only those who love you, why should you be rewarded? Don't even publicans do the same? And if you greet only your brothers, how are you different from any other person? Don't the publicans do the same?

You are to be perfect, just as your Father in heaven is perfect.

— Matthew 5

When you give to the poor, take care that you do not do so in front of others, so that they will see you; in that case you will have no reward from your Father in heaven. When you give to the poor do not sound a trumpet first, as hypocrites do in the synagogue and on the street, so that people will praise them. Truly, they already have their reward. When you give alms, do not let your left hand know what your right hand is doing; that way your generosity is a secret, and your Father, who sees all that is done secretly, will reward you.

When you pray do not be like the hypocrites, who love to be seen praying in the synagogues and on street corners. Truly, they already have their reward. When you pray, go into your room privately, close the door, and pray secretly to your Father. Your Father, who sees what is secret, will reward you.

When you pray, do not keep repeating your prayer uselessly, as pagans do, because they believe that all this talk will win them a hearing. Do not be like this, because your Father knows what you need before you ask him.

This is the way you should pray:

Father in heaven, may your name be called holy.

May your kingdom come. May your will be done on earth, as it is done in heaven. Give us today the bread we need. Forgive us the wrong we have done, as we forgive those who have done wrong to us. Do not let us be tempted, but deliver us from the evil one.

If you forgive others the wrong they have done, your Father in heaven will forgive you as well. But if you do not forgive them, your Father in heaven will not forgive you.

You should have the same attitude towards fasting. Do not look sad or make your face disfigured to let others know you are fasting, the way hypocrites do. Truly, they already have their reward. When you fast, anoint your head and wash your face, so that no one will know you are fasting. Your Father who sees what is done secretly will know, and he will reward you.

Do not store up the goods of this world; moth and rust will wear them away, and thieves can break in and steal them. Instead, lay up treasure for yourself in heaven, where moth and rust can't wear them away, or thieves break in and steal. Where your treasure is, your heart will be.

The light of the body is the eye. If your eye is whole, you will be filled with light. But if your eyes are bad your whole body is plunged into darkness. If you do not have light but darkness, how great is that darkness!

No man can serve two masters. He will hate one and love the other, or he will be loyal to one and despise the other. You cannot serve God and Mammon.

Therefore I tell you, do not be anxious about your life, what you will eat and drink; or for your body, what you will wear — after all, life is more than meat, the body is more than clothes. Learn from the birds of the air: they don't sow or reap or store up grain, and still your heavenly Father feeds them. Aren't you greater than that? Which of you, by being anxious about it, can add a foot to his height? And why worry about clothes? Learn from the lilies of the field and the way they grow. They do not work hard or spin thread, and yet Solomon in all of his royal splendor was not dressed so beautifully. If God dresses the grass of the field so wonderfully (grass which is here today and burnt tomorrow) will he not clothe you even more wonderfully, you who have so little faith? Do not worry, asking, "What are we to eat? What will we drink? What will we wear?" Gentiles worry over those things, but your heavenly Father knows that you need all of them. Your search should be first of all for God's Kingdom and his justice; all the rest will be taken care of.

So don't worry about what will happen tomorrow; tomorrow will take care of itself. Each day has its own problems.
— Matthew 6

Do not judge, so that you will not be judged; you will be judged in the way you have judged others, and what you measure out to others will be measured out to you. Why do you pay attention to the speck of dust in your brother's eye, but ignore the board in your own? How can you say to your brother, "Let me take that speck out of your eye," while the board is in your own? Hypocrite — first throw out the board in your own eye, and then you will be able to see clearly enough to remove the speck in your brother's eye.

Do not give what is holy to dogs, or cast your pearls before swine; they will trample them under their feet, and then turn to you, and tear you apart.

Ask and it will be given to you. Seek, and you will find. Knock, and it will be opened to you. For everyone who asks, receives, and he who seeks, finds, and he who knocks, has it opened for him. Which one of you, if his son asks for bread, will give him a stone? Or if he asks for a fish, will give him a serpent? If you, then, evil as you are, know how to give good gifts to your children, how much more will your Father in heaven give good gifts to those who ask him.

All of those things which you would like others to do to you, do to them. This is the law and the prophets.

Enter the narrow gate. It is the wide gate and the broad road that lead to destruction, and many go that way. But the small gate and the narrow road lead to life, and few find it.

Beware of the false prophets, who come to you looking like sheep, though inwardly they are hungry wolves. You will know them by their fruits. Do people gather grapes from thorns, or figs from thistles? In the same way, every good tree produces good fruit, but a blighted tree produces bad fruit. A good tree cannot produce bad fruit, nor can a bad tree produce good fruit. Every tree which does not produce good fruit is chopped down and burned. So it is by their fruits that you will know them.

Not everyone who says, "Lord, Lord," to me will enter into the kingdom of heaven; that is for the one who does the will of my Father in heaven. On that day many will say to me, "Lord, Lord, haven't we prophesied in your name? In your name didn't we cast out devils, and do many other wonderful things?" Then I will say to them, "I never knew you. Leave me, all of you evil-doers."

Therefore whoever hears my teaching and does what it says, is like a wise man who built his house on rock. The rain poured, floods came, wind blew, beating at his house, but it was built on rock and did not fall. Everyone who hears my teaching and does not do what it says, is like a foolish man who built his house on sand. The rain poured, the floods came, and winds blew, beating at the house; it fell, and how great was its fall! — Matthew 7

Give, and you will have gifts given to you — good measure, pressed down, shaken together, and overflowing into your lap! What you give out to others will be given to you in return. — Luke 6:38

The disciple is not above his master; but everyone who is perfected will be like his master. — Luke 6:40

Understand this: it is not what goes into a man's mouth that defiles him, but that which comes out of his mouth. — Matthew 15:10-11

Don't you understand that whatever enters the mouth goes into the stomach, and from there to the sewer? But the things which come out of the mouth come from the heart. They defile a man, because it is from the heart that evil thoughts, murders, adultery, fornication, thefts, lies, and blasphemies come. These are the things which defile a man; but eating with unwashed hands does not defile a man.
— Matthew 15:17-20

Sell everything you have and give it to the poor. Provide yourselves with purses which do not grow old, and a treasure in heaven which does not run out; no thief can come near it, no moth can consume it. Where your treasure is, your heart will be.

Be ready, with belt fastened and lights burning. Be like men who wait for their master's return from a wedding party, so that when he comes and knocks they can open the door immediately to let him in. Happy are those servants whose master finds them waiting. I tell you he will fasten his own belt, ask them to take their seats, and serve them himself! — Luke 12:33-37

There is nothing covered up which will not be revealed, nothing hidden which will not be made known. What you speak during the night will be heard in daylight; what you have whispered secretly will be proclaimed from the rooftops. My friends, I tell you, do not be afraid of those who can kill the body. After that there is nothing more they can do. I will tell you the one to fear: fear the one who, after he has killed you, can cast you into hell. Yes, I tell you, fear him. Aren't five sparrows sold for two small coins? God does not forget one of these birds. Even the hairs on your head are counted! So do not be afraid: you are worth more than many sparrows.   — Luke 12:2-7

The gospel of John presents a picture of Jesus which is so different from that offered by Matthew, Mark, and Luke that it seems at times to be about a different character. In the first three gospels Jesus' revelation of himself as Messiah is gradual, and it is never claimed that the Messiah is divine (though his role is certainly of divine origin). In John we find Jesus claiming to be the Messiah, the chosen one, from the start, and we find an even more startling claim: "Before Abraham was, I am." "The Father and I are one."

How can we explain these differences? The intention of the gospel of John is different from that of Matthew, Mark, and Luke. John's gospel presents a theological view of Jesus, as he is present in the life of the church. So, although John does not discuss the baptism of Jesus, he does speak of the need for the baptism of Christians. And although there is no account of the eucharist celebrated at the last supper, there is a long passage about Jesus, "the bread of life," and the necessity of receiving that bread.

In the first three gospels we find the story of Jesus and his teaching. In John we find the interior life of Jesus, and of the church. John's gospel, and the writings of Paul, are the beginning of Christian theology. In the early church John was called "John the theologian". In our time theology is often seen as a dry, unnecessarily academic approach to something which can't be spoken about at all, and the writings of theologians too often bear this out. In John we see theology as it should be done: prayerfully, out of a deep silence which knows the presence of the risen Lord.

I tell you, unless a man is born again he cannot see the Kingdom of God. Unless a man is born again of water and the spirit, he cannot enter the Kingdom of God. What is born of flesh is flesh, and what is born of the Spirit is spirit. Do not be surprised because I tell you, "You must be born again." The wind blows wherever it wills, and you hear the sound of it, but you do not know where it comes from or where it goes. So it is with everyone born of the Spirit.

I tell you, we speak what we know, and bear witness to what we have seen, and yet you do not accept this witness. If you do not believe what I tell you about earthly things, how will you believe if I tell you about the things of heaven?

No man ever went up to heaven except the one who came down from heaven, the Son of Man who lives in heaven. Just as Moses lifted up the serpent in the wilderness, so the Son of Man must be lifted up, so that everyone who believes in him will have eternal life.

God loved the world so much that he gave up his only Son, so that everyone who believes in him will not die but have eternal life. God did not send his Son into the world to condemn it, but that through him the world might be saved. He who believes in him will not be condemned, but he who does not believe is already condemned, because he has not believed in the name of the only Son of God.

This is the condemnation: light has come into the world, and men loved darkness rather than light, because their deeds were evil. Everyone who does evil hates the light, and will not come near the light, afraid that his deeds will be revealed. But he who lives truly comes into the light, and it is revealed that his works are the works of God.
— John 3:3-21

Here Jesus speaks to Nicodemus, a wise Pharisee who came secretly to Jesus to learn what his teaching meant. He is perplexed (understandably) when Jesus tells him he must be born again. The new birth which Jesus speaks about is the new life which follows repentance and baptism. This life takes the believer close to the life of God; his own life is animated by God's life. The flesh and spirit here are not opposed — flesh is life seen as a merely worldly thing. Spirit is the life that God gives; in Greek the words for "breath" and "spirit" are the same. In Genesis it is the breath of God which brings life to Adam; it is God's spirit which is the life of the believer. The fullness of that life has been revealed in Jesus, who will, like the bronze serpent described in Numbers 21, be "lifted up" as a sign of salvation. This "lifting up" has a double meaning: Jesus will be exalted by the Father in his resurrection and ascension into heaven; but first he will be lifted up on the cross.

You seek me out not because you have seen the great works I do; no, but because you ate the bread and were filled. Do not work for food which spoils, but for the food which brings everlasting life, which the Son of Man will give you. God the Father has placed on him his seal of authority.

The work which God wants you to do is to believe in the one he has sent.

I tell you, Moses gave you bread, but it was not from heaven. My Father gives true bread that comes from heaven. The bread of God is the one who comes down from heaven, bringing life to the world.

I am the bread of life. He who comes to me will not hunger, and he who believes in me will never thirst. But as I have said, you do not believe even though you have seen.

All that the Father gives me will come to me, and I will not leave anyone who comes to me.

I have come from heaven not to do my own will, but the will of him who sent me. And this is the will of my Father who sent me: that I should not lose any out of all he has given me, but raise them up on the last day.

This is the will of him who sent me: that everyone who sees the Son, and believes in him, will have everlasting life, and I will raise him up again on the last day.

No one can come to me unless the Father who sent me draws him; and I will raise him up on the last day. The prophets write, "And they shall all be taught by God." So everyone who has listened and learned from the Father comes to me. Not that anyone has seen the Father. Only he who comes from the Father has seen the Father.

I tell you the truth: whoever believes in me has everlasting life.

I am the bread of life.

Your fathers ate manna in the desert, and they are dead. The bread which comes down from heaven is such that a man may eat it, and never die. I am the living bread which comes from heaven. If anyone eats this bread he will live forever.

The bread I will give is my flesh; I give it for the life of the world.

What I tell you is true: unless you eat the flesh of the Son of Man and drink his blood, you have no life in you. Whoever eats my flesh and drinks my blood has eternal life, and I will raise him up on the last day.

My flesh is real food, and my blood is real drink. He who eats my flesh and drinks my blood lives in me, and I in him. As the living Father has sent me, and I live with his life, so he who eats me will live with my life. This is the bread which comes down from heaven: not like the manna which your fathers ate, and then died; he who eats this bread will live forever.

Do you find this shocking? What if you see the Son of Man ascend to the place he was before? The Spirit alone can give life; the flesh is of no use. The words I speak to you are spirit and life. — John 6:26-63

This, John tells us, was considered so difficult to accept that many of his followers left him. Jesus seemed to be calling for a strange, symbolic cannibalism, and claiming the authority to mediate God's creative, life-giving power. The wild symbolism of the eucharist is too easily lost on us, because we are so familiar with it. It shouldn't take much meditation on the subject to bring us to some realization of how shocking this must have seemed to those who first heard it. But the twelve stayed with Jesus because, in Peter's words, he had "words of eternal life." Their faith, which lasted in the face of this dreadful and difficult teaching, kept them with him. And it is faith, the belief in Jesus and his mission, which makes it possible to take this bread and wine, and make it flesh and blood. It is the action of God, his Spirit, which gives life, which makes the bread and wine become for us Jesus' body and blood. Faith has to precede our participation in the Lord's supper; without faith it will not help us. To use a homely metaphor, eating fish will not make us more fish-like. To partake of bread and wine at a eucharistic celebration, without faith, is a meaningless gesture, an outward thing, part of the world defined by Jesus as "the flesh which is of no use."

If anyone thirsts let him come to me and drink. As scripture says, he who believes in me "will have streams of living water flowing from within him." — John 7:37-38

Jesus speaks to the Samaritan woman of the water of life. This never-ending spring, a source of life, is something which Jesus brings to the faithful, and they in turn are sources of life for those with whom they come in contact.

I am the light of the world. He who follows me will not walk in darkness, but will have the light of life.
— John 8:12

If you live in my word, then you are truly my followers. You will know the truth, and the truth will make you free.
— John 8:31-32

I am not possessed. I honor my Father, but you do not honor me. I do not look for my own glory. There is one who does, and he passes judgement. What I tell you is true: if a man lives according to my teaching, he will not die.
— John 8:49-51

He who believes in me believes not in me, but in him who sent me. He who sees me sees him who sent me. I have come as light to the world, so that whoever believes in me will not live in darkness. And if someone hears my words and does not believe, I do not judge him; I did not come to judge, but to save the world. He who rejects me and refuses my teaching has a judge — my teaching, which will judge him on the last day. I have not spoken of my own accord. The Father who sent me told me what to say and how to speak. I know his commands are eternal life. Therefore, I say whatever he tells me to say.
— John 12:44-50

Now the Son of Man is glorified, and God is glorified in him. If God is glorified in him, God will also glorify him in himself, and he will glorify him now.
— John 13:31-32

I give you a new commandment: Love one another. As I have loved you, love one another. In this way all will know that you are my disciples.
— John 13:31-35

We are told to love one another as Jesus loved us, and his love was the love of God himself. In other words, we are asked to act towards one another as God acts towards us: with a love which stops at nothing and knows no limits. Obviously this is not within our power. That is the whole point: only if we accept the life which God offers in Jesus are we able to act as God asks us to. If we do accept that gift, his life, we are able to bring God to one another.

> The light is with you only a little while. Walk while the light lasts, or darkness may come upon you. He who walks in darkness does not know where he is going. While you have light, believe in the light, so that you may be children of light.
> — John 12:35-36

> The hour has come for the Son of Man to be glorified. I tell you the truth: unless the grain of wheat falls into the ground and dies, it remains alone. But if it dies, it brings forth much fruit.
> He who loves his life will lose it, and he who hates his life in this world will keep it for life everlasting.
> If any man would be my servant, let him follow me. Where I am, my servant will be. If any man is my servant, my Father will honor him.
> Now I am troubled at heart, but what shall I say? Father, save me from this hour? But this hour is the reason I came.
> Father, glorify your name.
> — John 12:23-28

John says that at this moment a voice came from heaven, saying, "I have glorified it, and will glorify it again." Jesus knows that he must suffer and die, and feels anguish. Here and elsewhere in the Gospel we must face the deep sadness of Jesus. Those who make Christianity a cheery, consoling thing must remember that it was not so for Jesus. He knows that he must die, and lets his followers know that they also must empty themselves in order to receive God's life. Jesus himself, troubled as he is, accepts the will of the Father although something in him would rather not; and as he accepts it wholeheartedly the heavens open with God's voice.

> This voice came not for me, but for you. Now is the time of the world's judgement. Now the prince of this world will be cast out. And I, if I am lifted up from the earth, will draw everyone to me.
> — John 12:31-32

The reign of evil, the power which it has had, ends with Jesus' death, and his rising. Again there is the twofold meaning of "if I am lifted up." His crucifixion redeems us, and in ascending to the Father he is revealed as Lord of the universe. As Paul says, "He is the image of the invisible God . . . all things are held together in him." (Colossians 1)

> My kingdom does not belong to this world. If my kingdom were worldly, my followers would fight to defend me now. But my kingship comes from another place.
>
> You call me a king. The reason I was born, and came into the world, was to bear witness to the truth. Everyone who is of the truth hears my voice.
>
> — John 18:34-37

These words of Jesus to Pilate emphasize once more the starkness of the message Jesus brings. It is not a question of ordinary worldly concerns — it is much more than that, a choice between truth and falsehood, darkness and light. A king is a small thing, next to the person who bears witness to the truth. The truth which Jesus preached — which he *was* — is the whole meaning of the universe: the unbounded love of God, who is truth and light. To choose anything else, knowingly, is to choose falsehood.

On the night before he died Jesus shared the Passover meal with his followers. There he told them, in words more plain than they were accustomed to hearing from him, of his own relationship to the Father, and his relationship to them, a relationship which brought them into the life and love which the Father and Son share.

> Do not let your heart be troubled. You believe in God — believe in me as well. There are many dwelling places in my Father's house; I would have told you if this were not so. I go to prepare a place for you. And if I go to prepare a place for you, I will come again and take you to myself, so that you may be where I am. You know where I go, and you know the way there.
>
> I am the way, the truth, and the life. No one comes to the Father without me. If you knew me you would know my Father as well. From now on you know him, and have seen him.
>
> Have I been with you all this time, and still you do not know me? He who has seen me has seen the Father; so how can you ask, "Show us the Father"? Don't you believe that I am in the Father, and the Father is in me? The words I speak to you are not my own; it is my Father dwelling within me who works. Believe me: I am in the Father, and the Father is in me; or believe because of the works themselves.
>
> I tell you truly that the one who believes in me will do what I do; indeed, he will do even greater things, because I am going to my Father. Whatever you ask in my name I will do, so that the Father may show

his glory in the Son. If you ask anything in my name, I will do it.

If you love me, keep my commandments; and I will pray to the Father, and he will give another Advocate to you, who will stay with you forever. This is the Spirit of Truth. The world cannot receive him, because it does not see or know him. But you know him, because he lives with you and will be in you.

I will not leave you without comfort — I will come to you. In a short time the world will see me no more. But you will see me; because I live you will also live. On that day you will know that I am in my Father, and you in me, and I in you.

He who hears my commandments and keeps them, he is the one who loves me. He who loves me will be loved by my Father, and I will love him, and will reveal myself to him.

If a man loves me he will keep my words, and my Father will love him. We will come to him, and make our home with him. But he who does not love me does not keep my words.

The word you hear is not mine. It is the Father's, and he sent me.

I have told you these things while I am with you. But the Advocate, the Holy Spirit whom the Father will send to you, will teach you all things, and recall for you all the things I have said to you.

Peace I leave you, my peace I give to you — I give it to you as the world never could. Do not let your hearts be troubled or afraid.

You have never heard me say to you, I will go away and come to you again. If you loved me you would rejoice that I am going to the Father, for my Father is greater than I.

I have told you this before it happens, so that when it does happen you will believe. I will not speak much longer — the prince of this world is coming. He cannot rule me, but the world must know that I love my Father, and what the Father has commanded I will do.   — John 14

I am the true vine, and my Father is the gardener. He cuts away every branch which bears no fruit, and he cleans the fruit-bearing branches so that they will yield more fruit. You have been cleaned through the word that I spoke to you.

Live in me, as I live in you. Just as the branch cannot bear fruit by itself, unless it lives with the vine, so you cannot unless you live in me.

I am the vine, you are the branches. The one who lives in me, and I in him, brings forth much fruit. Without me you can do nothing.

If someone does not live in me he is like a separate branch: he withers. Men gather branches, throw them into the fire, and burn them.

If you live in me, and my words live in you, you will ask what you will, and it will be done for you. Thus my Father will be glorified: you will bear much fruit, and be my disciples. As the Father has loved me, I love you. Continue living in my love. If you keep my commandments you will live in my love, just as I keep my Father's commandments and live in his love.

I have said these things to you so that my joy might remain in you, to make your joy full.

This is my commandment: love one another as I have loved you.

A man can show no love greater than the love it takes to lay down his life for his friends. You are my friends, if you do what I command. From now on I do not call you servants; a servant does not know what his master does. Instead I call you friends, because I have revealed to you everything I have heard from my Father.

You have not chosen me, but I have chosen you and charged you: you are to go and bear fruit, fruit which will last, so that my Father will give you anything you ask in my name.

I command you to love one another.

If the world hates you, remember: it hated me first. If you belonged to the world, the world would love its own; but I have chosen you out of the world, and it does not own you. Therefore it hates you.

Remember what I told you: the servant is not greater than his master. If they have persecuted me, they will persecute you. They will follow your teaching the way they followed mine. They will treat you this way because of me, because they do not know the One who sent me.

If I had not come and spoken to them, they would not have sinned. But now their sin has no cover. He who hates me hates my Father.

If I had not done works no other man has done while I was among them, they would not have sinned. But seeing my works they have hated me, and my Father. This has happened in fulfillment of scripture, which says, "They have hated me without cause."

But when the Advocate comes, whom I will send from the Father — the Spirit of Truth, who proceeds from the Father — he will be a witness for me. You are also to be witnesses, because you have been with me from the beginning.

— John 15

I have spoken these things to forewarn you. They will expel you from the synagogue, and the time comes when the person who kills you will believe that he does God a service. They will do these things to you because they have not known the Father, or me.

I have told you these things so that you will remember them when they come to pass. At first I did not tell you these things, because I was to be with you for awhile. But now that I am going away to him who sent me, no one asks me, "Where are you going?" although you are all grieving over the things I tell you. All the same, the truth is that it is for your sakes that I leave. If I do not leave, your Advocate will not come to you. But if I leave you, I will send him to you. And when he has come, he will show the world what sin, righteousness, and judgement mean. Sin: because they do not believe in me. Righteousness: because I go to my Father, and you will not see me. Judgement: because the prince of this world is condemned.

I still have many things to say to you, but you would find them unbearable now. However, when the Spirit of Truth has come he will guide you into all truth. The words he speaks will not be his own; he will speak what he hears, and will show you things to come. He will glorify me, and everything he reveals to you will come from me. All that the Father has is mine; this is why I said that everything he reveals to you will come from me.

In a little while you will not see me; and again, in a little while, you will see me once more, because I go to the Father. Do you wonder what this means? I tell you the truth: you will weep and lament while the world rejoices. You will be sorrowful — but your sorrow will turn to joy. A woman who goes through the pains of childbirth is in sorrow, because her hour has come. But once she has given birth she forgets her anguish and rejoices at the child who has been born into the world. So now you have sorrow; but I will see you again, and your heart will rejoice with a joy which cannot be taken from you. On that day you will ask nothing of me. I tell you truly that whatever you ask the Father in my name, he will grant. Up to this point you have asked for nothing in my name. Now ask, and you will receive, and your joy will be full.

I have told you these things in proverbs. But the time is coming, when I will not speak to you in proverbs; I will show you the Father's truth plainly. At that time you will ask in my name, and I do not say that I will pray to the Father for you; the Father himself loves you, because you loved me, and you believed that I came from God. I came from the Father, into the world. Now I leave the world, to go to the Father.

You believe all of this, you think. But the hour is coming — in fact it is here — when you will be scattered, each going his own way, leaving me alone. Yet I am not alone, because the Father is with me.

I have told you these things so that you might find peace in me. You will face many trials in the world. But be of good cheer: I have overcome the world.
— John 16

JESUS' PRAYER FOR US

Father, the hour has come. Glorify your Son, that the Son may glorify you. You have given him power over everyone, to give eternal life to those you have given him.

This is eternal life: to know that you alone are truly God, and to know Jesus Christ, whom you have sent.

I have glorified you on earth. I have finished the work which you gave me to do. Now, Father, glorify me with your own life, with the glory I shared with you before time began.

I have shown your name to the men you gave me out of the world. They were yours; you gave them to me, and they have kept your word. Now they know that you have given me all that is yours. I have told them what you have told me, and they have received your word. Now they are certain that I came from you. They believe that you sent me.

I pray for them. I do not pray for the world, but for those you have given me, because they are yours.

All of those who are mine are yours, and yours are mine, and I am glorified in them.

Now I am not in the world. But they remain in the world, as I come to you. Holy Father, protect those whom you have given me with the power of your name, that they may be one, as we are one. While I was with them in the world I kept them from evil through the power of your name. I kept all of those you gave me from evil, losing no one except the one who was fated to be lost, for the fulfillment of scripture.

I come to you now, saying these things in the world so that my joy might fill them.

I have given them your word, and the world has hated them, because they are not of the world, just as I am not of the world. I do not pray that you take them from the world, but that you keep them from evil. They are not of the world, as I am not of the world. Sanctify them through your truth: your word is truth.

As you sent me into the world, so I send them into the world; and I consecrate myself for their sakes, so that they may also be consecrated through the truth.

It is not only for them that I pray, but also for those who will come to believe in me because of their word, that all may be one, as you, Father, are in me, and I in you — that they may be one in us, so that the world will believe that you have sent me.

The glory which you gave me I have given them so that they may be one, as we are one: I in them, and you in me, all of them perfected as one. Then the world will know that you have sent me, and that you have loved them, as you loved me.

Father, I want these, your gift to me, to be with me where I am, to behold my glory, your gift to me, given in love before time began. Good Father, the world has not known you. But I know you, and these men know that you sent me. I have told them your name, and I will tell it, so that the love which you have for me will be in them, and I will be in them.

— John 17

Jesus' last words to his assembled followers occupy a greater place in John's gospel than in the first three gospels, and there is a combined poignancy and urgent instruction in his words. It may be irreverent to approach this gospel scene as you would a scene in a novel or movie, but it may be just as callous and insensitive *not* to. When at several points Jesus seems to underscore the lack of comprehension the apostles have brought to his tragedy — when, for instance, he asks, "do you understand what this means? . . . You believe all of this, you think, but you will be scattered and leave me alone . . . " — his isolation is terrible, and it begins with the fact that *no one* seems to understand his message, not even his friends; it ends with the feeling that even his Father has forsaken him on the cross. The horror of incarnation is that God forsakes God, taking on all the agony of being flesh, the suffering and uncertainty which mortality implies; and the God who is willing to go through the agony of death is the same One who raises suffering flesh from death to divinity, who shares divine life with what would decay without God's unlimited and impossible love. The God who can bridge the gap from the absolute unknowable to the fact of flesh is the God of all, the God of living and dead, imcomprehensible and still willing to be comprehended, loving enough to be flesh and blood, to let us know that the poles of love are as particular as blood and bread, and are also incomprehensible.

If this had happened once in history it would be enough. But the gospel of John goes further. "As the Father sent me, I send you . . . if they have done this to me, they will do it to you . . . you will do what I have done, even greater things . . . " Paul's epistles stress the early Christian belief that Jesus, in rising from the dead, was the first-born of many brothers and sisters, and it is this teaching which Jesus' last words to his disciples underscore: we are to be what Jesus was. As the Fathers of the church stress, to keep us in our place, we are not gods by nature, but gods by adoption. In a time which is willing to reduce men and women and children to ashes, it is important to remember that we are called on to be divine.

THE LAST THINGS

Early Christians expected Jesus to return in messianic splendor, perhaps within their own lifetime. Jesus himself appears to have shared the belief that the messianic age would begin quite soon, and Paul also mentions it in several places. But after several generations passed and the world remained, unreconciled and to all appearances unredeemed, Christians tended to underplay the apocalyptic element of Christianity. They began to see the last things in personal terms; these warnings apply to the individual, and he will be confronted with his responsibility for his life at death, when he meets God, and again at the end of time, at the time of the resurrection from the dead. "The end of time" became an abstract idea. Presumably it would be far in the future . . . and thank God for that. However and whenever it happened, it was no longer a major concern. The judgement which happened at death was the one which mattered, and the "general judgement" was added as an afterthought, almost. You knew you had it made (if you had been saved) and getting your body back was a bonus. If you hadn't made it, things could hardly be worse anyway.

I don't mean to mock this attitude, but it was one which strays so far from scripture and the faith of the first Christians that we must not be complacent about accepting our amended version. The parable of the last judgement in Matthew 25 (see page 65) tells part of the story of the last things; so do the passages below.

> You cannot tell by looking when the Kingdom of God will come. They will not say, "Look! Here!" or "There it is!" For the fact is that the Kingdom of God is within reach.
> The time will come when you will long to see one of the days of the Son of Man, and you will not see it. They will say to you, "Here it is!" or "There!" Do not go off after them.
> Just as lightning flashes instantly from one side of the sky to the other, so will it be on the day of the Son of Man. People ate, drank, and married, until the day Noah entered the ark. Then the flood came, and destroyed them all. So it was in Lot's time. They ate, drank, bought, sold, planted and built — but on the day Lot left Sodom, fire and brimstone rained from heaven and destroyed them all.
> This is how it will be on the day when the Son of Man is revealed.
> On that day, if a man is on his rooftop and his belongings are inside the house, he should not go in to get them; the person in the field shouldn't turn back to his house. Remember Lot's wife.
> Whoever tries to save his life would lose it. Whoever loses his life will save it.
> In that night, I tell you, two men will be in bed. One will be taken, the other left. Two women will be grinding together. One will be taken, the other left. Two men will be in the field, and one will be taken, the other left.
> Where the body lies, vultures gather.   — Luke 17:20-37

Although Jesus himself names signs of the coming of the kingdom, he warns that you cannot determine "it is here" or "there." It is (depending on which of the several existing early manuscripts you read) "within you," or "among you" or "within reach." It is close at hand, it has begun to make itself known through Jesus, but it will come to fulfillment suddenly, unpredictably.

> Be careful that no one deceives you. Many will come in my name, saying, "I am the Christ," and, "the Day is near." Do not follow them.

When you hear of wars and disturbances, do not be frightened. First these things must happen, but this is not yet the end.

Nation will rise up against nation, and kingdom war on kingdom, and there will be great earthquakes in many places, and famines, and plagues. There will be fearful sights and great omens in the skies.

But before this happens they will seize you, persecute you, hand you over to the synagogues and put you in prison. You will be brought before kings and rulers because you are with me. This will be your opportunity to testify. But be sure not to think beforehand of what you will answer. I will give you the words and the wisdom, which all of your enemies will be unable to deny or resist. You will be betrayed by parents, brothers, family, and friends, and they will put some of you to death. Because of me, you will be hated by everyone. But not one hair of your head will perish. Your endurance will win your life.

When you see Jerusalem surrounded by armies, know that the desolation of Jerusalem is near. Then let those in Judea run to the mountains, and those who are in the city must leave, and those who are in the country must not enter it. These are the days of vengeance, and everything written will be fulfilled. But woe to those who are pregnant, and to nursing mothers, during those days! The distress will be great throughout the land, and there will be a terrible judgement on this people. They will be slaughtered with swords; they will be led into other lands, captive. Jerusalem will be trampled by the Gentiles, until they have had their day.

There will be signs in the sun, and the moon, and the stars. On earth turmoil and confusion will seize the nations, as the sea and waves roar, and men's hearts will faint with fear as they see what is happening to the earth, because the powers of heaven will be shaken.

Then they will see the Son of Man coming on a cloud, in power and glory.

When these things have happened, then you can look up, and lift your heads, because salvation comes near.

Look at the fig tree, and all trees. When they begin to bud, you know that summer is close at hand. When you see these things, you know that the Kingdom of God is very close.

What I tell you is true: this generation will not pass away until all this has come to be. Heaven and earth will pass away, but my words will not pass away.

Pay attention to your own lives, so that your hearts will not be distracted with luxurious living, drunkenness, and worry over day to day things; then that day might come upon you unexpectedly. It will close upon everyone who lives on the face of the earth, like a trap. So keep watch, and pray constantly, that you may be counted worthy to escape everything that is coming, and stand before the Son of Man.

— Luke 21:8-36

You will see the Son of Man sitting on power's right hand, coming on the clouds of heaven. — Mark 14:62

Be careful to watch and pray, because you do not know when the time will be. The Son of Man is like a man who took a journey far away, leaving his house in the hands of servants. Every one of them had his job to do, and he told the porter to keep watch.

So you should keep watch, because you do not know when the master of the house is coming, whether it will be in the evening, at midnight, when the cock crows, or during the morning. If he comes unexpectedly he might find you asleep. What I tell you, I tell to everyone: Watch. — Mark 13:33-37

Many of Jesus' predictions have to do with the fall of Jerusalem, which happened in the year 70 A.D. But others have to do with an even more shattering crisis. The day of the coming of the Son of Man was not itself the end of history; it was to usher in the reign of God which would reconcile everything in peace, under God's chosen leader, the Messiah. And this time was associated in the minds of early Christians with the fall of Jerusalem and the destruction of the Temple.

But we have to face the fact that our age, the time following the destruction of the Temple, hardly lives up to messianic expectations. Given the importance the expectation of the end had for early Christians, what are we to do with this fact? The solution of some fundamentalists is to point to the events we see going on around us as evidence of the imminent end of the world, omens of the second coming of Christ. But so many of the things they point to (earthquakes, wars, and famine) happen all the time, and before the last turn of the millenium, in the years immediately preceding the year 1000, many expected the end to come. The expectation of the end of history has been frustrated time and time again.

Without claiming that there will never be an end to history in this worldwide sense, at least an end which comes up to apocalyptic expectations, I think we can see these passages in another light. It might be a more relevant perspective, since it has to do with our lives in the world right now. Jesus ends his discourse on the day of the coming of the Son of Man with the warning, "watch." We must be alert for the coming of God, however it happens, and whenever. Jesus appeared to his followers as a stranger on several occasions after his resurrection, and he told them that whatever they did to the least person, they did to God. It is this alertness which remains necessary. It is part of the undivided allegiance which Christianity demands. It is not up to us to know the day or the hour — or even the condition. We may not put off the living of the Christian life until the signs of the time are foreboding, but must lose our lives, to gain them, now: moment to moment, day in and day out. The rest must be left to God.

The Hard Sayings

Many of the things which Jesus said are difficult to grasp, puzzling, bothersome. Anyone's selection of his most troublesome words would vary. The hardest words of all might be, "Love one another."

Still, some of Jesus' sayings are especially strange. They ring harshly, or seem to be so absolute and uncompromising that they could not possibly be spoken by anyone who was not a fanatic. Our first inclination is to interpret the force out of them; or we might apply them to anyone but ourselves. Our discomfort is forgiveable. If we had not been taught what we are to expect of Jesus, taught by our parents, or our church, or the Bible, we would believe that anyone who spoke this way was a fanatic.

Here are only some of the difficult sayings of Jesus. (Others may be found elsewhere throughout this book; and of course the New Testament is full of them.)

If anyone comes to me who does not hate his father, mother, wife, children, brothers and sisters — even his own life — he cannot be my follower. Whoever does not shoulder his cross and come after me cannot be my follower.

Which of you, wanting to build a tower, would not first sit down, and determine the cost, to make sure that he was able to complete it? If he does not do this, when a man has laid a foundation and is not able to finish the work, everyone who sees it will laugh at him, saying, "This man started to build but could not finish."

What king, going to make war against another, does not first sit down to see whether he can meet with ten thousand men an army of twenty thousand? If he cannot, he will, while there is still distance between them, send a messenger with peace conditions.

In the same way, if you will not leave everything you have, you cannot be my disciple.
— Luke 14:26-33

I have come to set the earth on fire, and how I wish it were already blazing! But there is a baptism I must undergo first, and I am in bonds until it is done!

Did you think I came to give the world peace? No, I tell you, not peace, but division: from now on a household of five will be split, three against two and two against three. The father will be against the son, and the son against the father. The mother against the daughter, and the daughter against the mother; the mother-in-law against the daughter-in-law, and the daughter-in-law against the mother-in-law.
— Luke 12:49-53

My mother and my brothers are those who hear the word of God and do it.
— Luke 8:21

The last answer was given to someone who told Jesus that his mother and brothers were waiting to see him. It seems to be a repudiation of family allegiances, something which is also found in his words about "hating" mother and father, wife and child. Some critics have pointed out that this, given the languages involved, may mean "anyone who does not love me more," rather than "hate", where hatred is viewed as a destructive thing, a loathing; but this may only move the problem an inch back without removing the basic harshness of the statement. There is no mistaking the final meaning: the disciple of Jesus must not allow *any* commitment, not even one to his or her family, to stand in the way of the commitment owed to Jesus. This is one of the differences between classical paganism and Judaism, and it should be remembered that the gospel was being preached in a world saturated with paganism. Paganism not only allowed divided allegiance; it encouraged it. Religion was a part of life, like politics and economics, for the pagan. For the Jew, and then for the Christian, it was all or nothing. Jesus was telling his followers that as new as this was, it was not a religion of the pagan sort. Their commitment to him and to his teaching must be wholehearted and undivided, which could very well lead to the most painful division.

This all or nothing approach to life was for the believer even more intensely to be applied in marriage. When his disciples balk at Jesus' teaching on marriage, he speaks of something even more difficult than the absolute commitment he asks.

> Haven't you read that in the beginning, God made them male and female? For this reason a man will leave his father and mother, and be joined to his wife, and the two of them will be one flesh? They are no longer two, but one. Therefore, what God has made one, men should not part.
> Because your hearts are hard, Moses allowed you to divorce your wives, but that is not the way it was from the beginning. I tell you, whoever puts his wife away (for any reason other than adultery) and marries another, commits adultery. — Matthew 19:4-9

The reaction of his followers to this statement is like a thousand old jokes: if you can't get out of a marriage, then being single is better! Jesus uses the moment to speak of an aspect of Christian discipline which will be the lot of some of his followers:

> Not everyone can take this to heart, except those who have been given it: there are some who cannot marry because they were born that way, and others who have been made incapable of marriage by men. But there are others who refuse to marry for the sake of the Kingdom of God. He who can hear this, let him hear it. — Matthew 19:11-12

Celibacy was not a rule, but a gift . . . a difficult one too, undertaken because of the urgency which the proclamation of the kingdom requires.

This urgency was combined with a harshness which we would often rather forget in thinking about Jesus; we prefer our religious leaders to be serene and infinitely tolerant. But there is nothing tolerant in Jesus' words about the religious leaders he encountered.

> Isaiah's prophecy about you hypocrites was true: "This people honors me with their lips, but their heart is far from me, because they teach as true doctrine the rules made by men." Leaving aside God's commandment, you maintain man-made traditions, concerning such things as the washing of pots and cups, and other similar things. You reject God's command in favor of your own tradition. Moses said, "Honor your father and mother," and, "Whoever curses his father or

mother should die." But you say, "If a man says to his father or mother, 'I have set aside what I would have given to you, and now it belongs to God,' then he does not need to do anything for them." So the tradition which you hand down invalidates God's word! You do many things this way.

— Mark 7:6-13

You Pharisees clean the outside of the cup and plate, but inside you are greedy and wicked. Fools — didn't the one who made the outside also make the inside? Give what you are able to give, and everything will be clean for you. Woe to you, Pharisees! You put a tithe on mint, rue, and other herbs, and forget about judgement and the love of God. This is what you should have paid attention to, without neglecting the others. Woe to you Pharisees, because you love the best seats in the synagogue, and love to have people greet you in public. Woe to you, scribes, Pharisees, hypocrites! You are like unmarked graves; the people who walk over them are not aware of what lies beneath.

Woe to you also, you lawyers, who saddle men with burdens too heavy for carrying, burdens which you would not lift a finger to lighten. Woe to you! You build monuments to the prophets your fathers killed, and by doing this show your approval of the deeds of your fathers. They killed them, you build the memorials. This is what the Wisdom of God said, "I will send prophets and messengers, and some of them will be persecuted and killed." This generation will answer for all the prophets' blood spilled from the beginning of time; all the blood spilled from Abel to Zechariah, who died between the altar and the sanctuary, will be demanded.

Woe to you, lawyers! You have taken the key of knowledge away. You will not enter yourself, and you prevent other people from entering.

— Luke 11:39-52

Generation of vipers, how can you, evil as you are, speak good things? The mouth speaks from the heart's fullness.

A good man brings good things from his heart's treasure. An evil man brings evil things from his evil treasure.

I tell you, every idle word spoken by men will have to be accounted for on judgement day. By your words you will be acquitted — or condemned.

— Matthew 12:34-37

Also for you, Chorazin! Alas, Bethsaida! If the great works done in you had been done in Tyre and Sidon, they would have repented long ago in sackcloth and ashes. I tell you it will be better on judgement day for Tyre and Sidon than for you. And you, Capernaum, you wanted to be lifted to the heights of heaven? You will be thrown into hell. If the great works done in you had been done in Sodom, it would still be standing. But I tell you, on judgement day it will be better for Sodom than for you. — Matthew 11:21-24

An evil, unfaithful generation looks for a sign. There will be no sign given to it but the sign of Jonah the prophet. Just as Jonah spent three days and nights in the belly of a fish, so will the Son of Man be three days and nights in the heart of the earth. On judgement day the men of Nineveh will rise, along with this generation. They will condemn it, because when Jonah preached to them they repented. But someone greater than Jonah is here. On judgement day the queen of the south will rise, along with this generation; she will condemn it because she came from far away to hear the wisdom of Solomon. But someone greater than Solomon is here. — Matthew 12:39-42

Every plant which my heavenly Father has not planted shall be uprooted. Let them alone. They are blind leaders of the blind, and if the blind lead the blind, both fall into the ditch. — Matthew 5:13-14

Haven't you ever read in the scriptures, "The stone which the builders rejected has become the cornerstone; this is the Lord's doing, and it is wonderful in our eyes"? I tell you, the kingdom of God will be taken from you and given to people who will bring forth its fruits.
Whoever falls on this stone will be broken — but whoever has it fall on him will be ground to a powder. — Matthew 21:42-44

I am with you a little while longer, and then I go to him who sent me. You will look for me, and will not be able to find me. You will not be able to come where I am. — John 7:33-34

You are from beneath, I am from above. You are of this world; I am not of this world. Therefore I have said you will die in your sins,

because if you do not believe that I am he, you will die in your sins.
— John 8:23-24

I came into this world for judgement, so that those who are blind might see, and those who see might be blinded. — John 9:39

If you were really blind you would not be sinful. But because you say, "We see," your sin remains. — John 9:41

Doesn't scripture say, "My house will be called by all nations the house of prayer?" But you have made it a robber's den. — Mark 11:17

    The idea that Jesus was "meek and mild" is contradicted by these words. Christians have frequently interpreted them as attacks upon the Jews; this has been the interpretation given especially to the dialogue in John's gospel between Jesus and the leaders of the Jews.
    And of course the religious leaders who opposed Jesus *were* Jews. But Christians have derived, I am afraid, a terrible and completely false comfort from this. Not only has an anti-Jewish interpretation of these passages been used to justify anti-Semitic acts throughout the Christian era, but Christians have failed to read them at any depth. Precisely the same charges can be leveled against the successful Christian church, with very little change. Note that Jesus does not take them to task for their Judaism, but for their retreat from a living and vital Judaism. He speaks of the legalistic way they approach their religion and says they should have as their main concern "judgement and the love of God," not the rules. But he says — and this is very significant — that the love of God should be foremost, "without neglecting the others"; that is, the rules should be observed, but in a living context. They should not be seen as ends in themselves. The leaders of Judaism in his day were, Jesus is saying, tone-deaf: they seemed to have no feeling for real religion, but were concerned over superficialities, and mired in a smug self-assurance. This was all the more apparent from their rejection of him and his teaching. They did not recognize his divine authority, yet claimed religious insight. They claimed to see, when they could not. If they were truly ignorant, Jesus says, they might be excused for this, but because of their pretense, their assurance that they knew God's will, they were doubly guilty.

All of this can — and must — be applied to Christianity. There is a religiosity which can stand in the way of true religion, a preoccupation with rules and rituals, an assurance that "we have all the answers" which is a modern duplicate of the religious situation Jesus faced. Perhaps the most chilling words here are these: "Every idle word spoken by men will have to be accounted for on judgement day. By your words you will be acquitted — or condemned." If we claim to be God's people, if we say that our mission is to live his word, we had better live up to it. There is nothing worse than a belief that we really *have* repented, and turned our hearts around, and now can hug that repentance to ourselves in satisfaction. This is not genuine repentance (which is an ongoing thing) but a mental trick.

Repentance is a life and death matter, as Jesus emphasized when told about a slaughter which Pilate had done.

Do you think that these Galileans suffered because they were more sinful than other Galileans? No. But unless you repent, you will also perish. Or the eighteen people who died in Siloam, when the tower fell on them — do you think they were more sinful than anyone in Jerusalem? No. But unless you repent, you will all perish. — Luke 13:2-5

It was a lack of repentance, the early Christians believed, which led to the fall of Jerusalem.

If you only knew today the way which would bring you peace! But is it hidden from your eyes. The days will come when your enemies will dig trenches around you, surround you on every side, and level you and everyone in the city. They will not leave one stone standing on top of another, because you did not know God's time when it came.

— Luke 19:41-44

Daughters of Jerusalem, do not weep for me. Weep for yourselves, and for your children. The days are coming in which they will say, "Happy are the barren, the wombs which never conceived, and the breasts which never nursed." Then they will say to the mountains, "Fall on us," and to the hills, "Cover us." If they do these things when the wood is green, what will be done when it is dry? — Luke 23:28-31

We know that the early church regarded the fall of Jerusalem as an event of cosmic importance; and we know that they saw in such a great upheaval a sign of the end of the old world. What relevance does it have for us today? It is as remote as the fall of Carthage. But here we see something of Christianity's prophetic nature. Jerusalem is everywhere; it exists in every country and city where people are willing to accept the divided allegiance which God will not accept. Jerusalem, meant to be the place of peace, is always turning into Babylon, the ancient symbol of overwhelming power and corruption.

When Jesus holds out such an uncompromising view of repentance, when he scores the religious leaders and predicts disaster, we react the way we do to the one we call (too comfortably) "the God of the Old Testament," as if this were not also the God of Jesus. The prophetic aspect of Christianity has always been the one we have been most uncomfortable with. There is some good reason for the discomfort — there is such a thing as false prophecy, and fanaticism is a religious sickness. We often tell ourselves that the picture of a God who would do these things to Jerusalem, or to any place which displeased him, is not a God we can believe in. But when we say this we are missing the point. There is a moral and religious equilibrium which is as necessary to our continued existence as human beings as air is. When it is too drastically upset, we destroy ourselves. Failure to repent is a decision to persist in illusion, and a person who lives in a dream-populated world will sooner or later encounter nightmares. To say that this is unjust is like saying that if I stick my hand into a fire and meet pain there, that is unjust. It has nothing to do with fairness; it is the way things are. Our vocation is to be prophetic in our own time. Christians ordinarily are quick to stand up to what they know to be violations of personal morality. They are concerned over a decline in family life, for example, and corruption in business. But there are other pervasive evils: the fact that our society depends on waste, and our economy requires people to want what they do not need; the divisions between rich and poor, and the misery of the destitute; the persistence of racism, and an easy acceptance of an ever-growing military power — all of these are signs of corruption and a lack of reconciliation. As even an agnostic can recognize, they are wounds in our common life. By living the life of the Kingdom, Christians can begin God's healing work.

The repentance Jesus asks for includes a turning away from our normal standards of judgement. Normally we see sinners as "other": we are not like that. Jesus tells us to love one another, and this includes forgiveness.

> Whoever among you is without sin, let him throw the first stone.
>
> — John 8:7

This does not mean that we cannot recognize sin: Jesus did, and forgave sinners. This means that we do not regard the sin of another as something which allows us to be separate from the sinner. Recognizing the sin in ourselves, we see in the sinner a sister, a brother, in need of healing just as we are.

> I tell you the truth: every sin can be forgiven any human being, even the worst blasphemy. But whoever blasphemes the Holy Spirit cannot be forgiven; he is in danger of eternal damnation.
>
> — Mark 3:28-29

What is the sin against the Holy Spirit? This passage has long been a difficult one. Jesus speaks specifically of those who attribute his work to the devil. The sin against the Holy Spirit in this context means a refusal to recognize the good work of God. To refuse to recognize God's power, to refuse God himself, makes even forgiveness impossible. God cannot work in us if we will not give him the freedom to do so.

In looking at all of Jesus' hard sayings we are sometimes tempted to undervalue them, to put the urgency of his preaching after the comfort it brings us. But it is the words which might contain what we most need to hear which make us uncomfortable. In this light it seems appropriate to close this section with another of Jesus' hard sayings:

> Whoever is ashamed of me and of my words before this unfaithful and wicked age, of him the Son of Man will be ashamed when he comes in the glory of his Father, with the holy angels.
>
> — Mark 8:34-38

As the Father sent me, so I send you

It is not enough for us to appreciate Jesus' life and teaching, his death and resurrection. Christianity is not a passive commitment. We are expected to live the life he brought us — to allow God's kingdom, his power over our lives, to grow in us; this means to share it. The words of instruction and encouragement which he gave to his followers apply to us as well, and we can learn from them what it means to be his people, his church. This is something that grows in us as we try to live it out; it isn't a given thing, obvious from the start. But we have his word, and the example of great Christians throughout the ages, as a testimony to the fact that if we try to follow him "we will not go without a reward."

When he gathered his first followers, a couple of them asked Jesus, "Rabbi, where do you live?" "Come and see," he answered. It is by coming to him that we begin to learn our work as Christians.

Follow me.
— Mark 2:14

Come with me, and I will make you fishers of men.
— Mark 1:17

Follow me, and let the dead bury their dead.
— Matthew 8:22

No man who has put his hand to the plow, but then looks back, is worthy of the Kingdom of God.
— Luke 9:62

Jesus makes it clear that following him is not something that can be done in a half-hearted manner. With him it is all or nothing; the commitment is a total one, or it is not real, and it means a leavetaking which is a complete turning around from our previous way of living. This "turning around" is the meaning of conversion. But as drastic a break as it is, it is one which should not discourage or frighten us.

> Why are you so fearful? Why do you have no faith?
> — Mark 4:40

> Do not be afraid — only believe.
> — Mark 5:36

> Be of good cheer — it is I. Do not be afraid.
> — Mark 6:50

> Be of good cheer. Your sins are forgiven.
> — Matthew 9:2

> Come to me, all you who work hard, whose burden is heavy: I will give you rest. Take my yoke upon your shoulders, and learn from me, because I am gentle and humble of heart, and you will find rest for your souls. My yoke is easy, my burden light.
> — Matthew 11:28-30

But what does it take to follow him? First, repentance. This is not just a turning away from everything which stands between us and God — it is a turning towards God, who gives us the power to accomplish it. This requires the gentleness and humility of Jesus, and we have his word for it that the burden will not be too great for us to bear. This humility is not a false, breast-beating sort. We should remember here that the word "humility" comes from "humus" — earth. It means getting a proper sense of proportion, true priorities, and our real place in the universe. It means, in a way, becoming earthy, learning a kind of commonness, the leaving behind of vanity and false glory to look for true glory. But we must first empty ourselves.

> If anyone wants to follow me, let him deny himself, take up his cross, and follow me. Whoever wishes to save his life will lose it, and whoever loses his life for my sake will find it. How is a man profited if

he gains the whole world — and loses his soul? What will a man give in exchange for his soul? For the Son of Man will come in his Father's glory with his angels, and then he will reward everyone according to his works. I tell you, there are some standing here who will not die until they see the Son of Man coming in his kingdom. — Matthew 16:24-28

Once when James and John quarrelled over the places they would have in the kingdom, Jesus made it clear that this is not the kind of reward his followers should expect:

You do not know what you ask. Can you drink the cup that I must drink? Or be baptized with the baptism I must undergo? Indeed, you will drink the cup I drink, and be baptized with the baptism I undergo; but to sit at my right hand and on my left hand is not mine to grant. It will be granted to those for whom it is prepared. — Mark 10:38-40

Jesus' followers may be expected to suffer as he did, but how God rewards them is not to be of concern. We do know that God loves us, and will do what is best for us. In that knowledge we should leave the rest to him.

When Jesus called Peter to follow him he accompanied his call with a wonderful sign.

Launch out into deep waters, and let down your nets for a catch.
— Luke 5:4

The catch was, of course, overwhelming. When Peter was confronted with this sign of the immense generosity of God, he fell to his knees before Jesus and said, "Leave me Lord, I am a sinner."

Do not fear. From now on you will catch men.
— Luke 5:10

This is how one becomes a follower of Jesus, someone who helps him spread the Kingdom. It begins with the confession of sin. But this is no neurotic grovelling. It is only next to the generosity of God that we can see our own smallness in proper perspective, and this smallness is sin. God's love for us is limitless. Compared to it, our love dwindles to nothing. Peter found himself confronted dramatically with this fact, and it shocked a confession of sin from him. Jesus' response was, "Do not fear." This encouragement is what should follow our realization of our own sinfulness. As Pascal wrote in *The Mystery of Jesus*, "As your sins are made known to you, they are forgiven." But this reconciliation is not something we are allowed to cherish in secret; we must forgive as we are forgiven.

If your brother does anything wrong to you, tell him that he has wronged you. If he repents, forgive him. And if he wrongs you seven times a day, and turns to you seven times, saying, "I repent," forgive him.
— Luke 17:1-4

This does not mean that the eighth time you have a right to refuse your brother; Peter asked if seven were the limit (probably thinking that seven was too great a strain on one's patience) and Jesus answered him,

Not only seven times — seventy times seven!
— Matthew 18:22

I send you out like sheep into the midst of wolves; so you must be as wise as serpents, and as innocent as doves. But beware: men will hand you over to councils, and scourge you in synagogues. You will be brought before governors and kings for my sake, to give testimony before them and before the Gentiles.
— Matthew 9:16-18

The disciple cannot expect more than the master, or the servant more than his lord. It is enough for the disciple to be like his master, and the servant to be like his lord. If they have called the master of the house "Beelzebub", what more will they say of his household?
— Matthew 9:24-25

The great harvest is ready, but the workers are few. So you must ask the lord of the harvest to send workers into the harvest fields. Go now: I send you like sheep into a pack of wolves.
Do not carry purse or pack, go barefoot, do not greet anyone along the way. When you go into a house, first say, "Peace be to this house." If the person who lives there is peaceful, your peace will rest there. If not, it will return to you. Stay in that house, taking whatever food they

give you. The worker earns what he works for. Do not move from house to house. Whatever city you go to, wherever you are made welcome, eat what they give you. Heal the sick, and say to the people, "God's Kingdom has come near you." When you go into a city and you are not welcomed, leave its streets. Say, "Even the dust of your city which clings to us we shake off as a sign against you. But realize this much: the Kingdom of God passed close by you." I tell you it will be better for Sodom than for that city when the day comes.
— Luke 10:2-12

Jesus stresses the urgency of spreading the word of the coming of the kingdom: his followers are to travel light, not even sparing the time to greet people they meet along the way. They have the power to communicate God's peace, where they encounter the willingness to accept it. They are to worry about nothing but the Kingdom. Where they are told to "eat what is set before them" the recommendation is not only one of simplicity and acceptance, the graciousness of the good guest; in addition, it means that even the normal Jewish dietary laws do not matter as much as the spreading of the news.

When I sent you without purse, pack, or shoes, did you ever need anything?
Now whoever has a purse should take it with him, as well as his pack, and whoever lacks a sword should buy one, even if he has to sell his coat to buy one. I tell you, what was written about me must be fulfilled: "He was counted among the outlaws." The things that concern me are coming true.
— Luke 22:35-37

This must have confused the disciples: it looked like a complete reversal of Jesus' earlier command. The one who, at another point in the New Testament, tells Peter, "Put away your sword: whoever lives by the sword will die by the sword", here tells the disciples to make sure they are armed. It is not a literal command. Jesus is not saying that where God once provided, and the disciples needed nothing, he will no longer provide. He says instead that the people he has called to himself will meet persecution. This apparent contradiction occurred just before his final suffering, when Jesus was threatened with arrest at any moment and knew that his followers, who often seemed so naive, were also faced with his fate. True to form, they do not see what he is saying. They have been taught to be peaceful, healing, compassionate, and now he says that they should arm themselves. They show him two swords, as if to ask if this is sufficient. Of course it would not be in any real military conflict, any truly violent confrontation; that was not Jesus' point. He answers with the weariness of an adult tired of children: "It is enough."

Toward the end of his life with us Jesus shows this isolation and weariness, followed by the joy of the resurrection — as if he were pleasantly, even ecstatically surprised by what God had in store for him. (This secret joy is one part of his humanity which at this point is closed to us. If he was truly "a man like us, in all things but sin," there are surprises he came to know as a man which we have yet to understand.) This delight was foreshadowed by his joy when his disciples returned from their mission.

I saw Satan fall like lightning from heaven! See: I give you power to tread scorpions underfoot, along with all the enemy's power. There is nothing that can ever harm you. But do not cherish the fact that spirits obey you. Instead, rejoice because your names have been written in heaven!
— Luke 10:18-20

Beware of the scribes who love the robes of their office, and the greeting they get from people in public, and the finest seat in the synagogue, and the finest place during the feasts. They eat up what widows have had left to them, and to satisfy superficial religiosity they make their prayers long. They will have the greatest punishment.
— Mark 12:38-40

Religiosity is the worst enemy of honest religion. The trappings of religion, the interesting decoration which so often surrounds it, can get in the way of what it is all about. Where religious institutions or the prestige of office become more important, the means become more important than the end, and the good news of the Kingdom becomes the interesting news of the interior decoration: frivolous and totally irrelevant.

The religion Jesus preached did not allow less than absolute commitment. It was more than an ethical thing; to follow him completely meant giving up everything, and for some people that is harder than it is for others. We are told that Jesus, looking upon the rich young man who wondered what he should do to have eternal life, "loved him," but the young man was unable to make the radical break which Jesus asked for.

    Why do you call me good? Only one is good; I am speaking of God. You know what is commanded: do not commit adultery, do not kill, do not steal, do not bear false witness, do not defraud, honor your father and mother.
    You lack one thing: go, sell whatever you own, give it to the poor, and you will have treasure in heaven. Come, and follow me.
— Mark 10:18-21

    Children, how hard it is for those who put their faith in riches to enter God's Kingdom. It is easier for a camel to go through a needle's eye than for a rich man to enter God's Kingdom.   — Mark 10:24-26

    When his followers realized how much each of them might, in Jesus' terms, be considered rich, they asked, "If that is the case, who can be saved?" Jesus' answer stresses God's mercy:

    With men it would be impossible, but not with God: with God all things are possible.   — Mark 10:27

    Jesus' followers believed that in Jesus they were free of the burden of the Jewish law, yet many of them continued to observe it, as Jesus had. In Matthew's gospel the story is told of an encounter Peter had with officials of the temple who asked whether Jesus had paid the temple tax. Knowing that Jesus observed the law although he did not feel bound by it, Peter answered that Jesus had. When Jesus next met Peter he had a question for him:

    Tell me, Simon: whom do the rulers of this world tax? Their own children, or strangers? The children are free. Nevertheless, we shouldn't give scandal. So go to the sea, throw out a line, and take the first fish which you catch. When you have opened his mouth you will find a coin; you can take it to them to pay for both you and me.
— Matthew 17:25-27

The independence of Jesus was sensed as a threat not only by religious authorities but by civil authorities as well, and this fact was used against him by his enemies on one occasion. Once they asked him if it was lawful for them to pay a tax levied by Rome. The tax was hated for political and religious reasons: Rome had colonized the country and the Roman presence was understandably resented. In addition the Roman coins in which the tax had to be paid bore the emperor's image — a violation of Jewish law, which did not allow representational images. (Under Pontius Pilate the Jews staged a protest against Pilate's use of banners bearing the emporer's image, and when even the threat of death failed to stop the protest Pilate backed down.) Jesus' enemies asked him about the tax in order to trap him: if he said that the tax was licit, he would alienate his Jewish followers. If he said it was not licit, he would be in trouble with the authorities. In his answer he forced his opponents to admit they themselves were less than scrupulous about paying the tax:

Why do you try to trap me? Bring me the coin of tribute and let me see it.
Whose image is this, and whose inscription?

They were able to bring him the coin because they themselves paid the tax. The trap was beginning to close, but not on Jesus. They told him that the image was Caesar's.

Then pay Caesar whatever belongs to Caesar, and pay God what is owed to God.
— Mark 12:15-17

This episode has been brought forth frequently as a scriptural proof that Christians have an obligation to civil authority. But, given its context, it is something else. What belongs to Caesar which does not first belong to God? It is not as if God and Caesar had divided the universe between them. What belongs to Caesar is insignificant; what belongs to God is everything. The effort to use this passage to argue for a divided allegiance is in effect a pagan thing, which would see life divided into "religious" and "non-religious" areas. One's allegiance to God must be single and total. Where Caesar makes a competing claim, the Christians must go against Caesar.

The Christian life must be rooted in prayer. Christian activity, Christian efforts at social renewal and reform, all the acts of the church are empty unless they begin in prayer, which is simply sanity. We are always in the presence of God. Prayer begins with the recognition of that fact. At times we need to get away from noise and distraction, creating a place in which everything can settle down and assume its real proportion. As urgent as the spreading of his teaching was, Jesus knew this and once told his followers,

> Come away with me, by yourselves, to a deserted place, where you can rest in peace.
> — Mark 6:31

> Martha, Martha, you worry and fret over so many things. But only one thing is necessary. Mary has chosen that good thing, and it will not be taken away from her.
> — Luke 10:41-42

Jesus said this when Martha, who was busy with her chores, complained that Mary simply sat listening to Jesus. This listening is the precondition for prayer. But there is more: prayer is also a matter of attitude, and Jesus told his followers the kind of prayer they should make:

> When you pray, say, "Our Father in heaven, hallowed be your name. Let your kingdom come, your will be done on earth, as it is in heaven. Give us each day the bread we need. Forgive us our sins, as we forgive those who have wronged us. Do not let us be tested, but deliver us from the evil one.
> — Luke 11:2-4

> Have faith in God. I tell you, whoever says to this mountain, "Move now, and throw yourself into the sea," and does not doubt, but believes that it will be so, he will have it happen as he says. So I say that whatever you want, when you pray, believe that you will receive them, and you will have them.
> And when you pray, if you have any grudge against anyone, forgive him. Then your Father in heaven will forgive you your wrongs. But if you do not forgive, your Father in heaven will not forgive your wrongdoing.
> — Mark 11:22-36

Everything is possible for the one who believes.

— Mark 9:23

If you had faith as small as a mustard seed, you could say to this sycamore, "Uproot yourself, and plant yourself in the sea," and it would obey you. But is there any one of you who will say to a servant who plows the field or feeds the cattle, when he has come in from the field, "Sit down and eat?" Wouldn't you say instead, "Bring me food, be alert and serve me, until I have had food and drink. You can eat and drink afterwards." Do you thank a servant for doing what he is required to do? Of course not. In the same way, when you have done all of these things that have been commanded, say, "We are servants who deserve nothing; we have done what was our duty."

— Luke 17:6-10

When Jesus met the Samaritan woman at the well and asked her for water, he spoke of the "living water" of faith.

If you could recognize God's gift, and who it is who asks you for something to drink, you would ask him instead, and he would give you living water.
Whoever drinks this well-water will be thirsty again. But whoever drinks the water I give him will never thirst again. The water I give will be a well of water springing up within him, into everlasting life.
Believe me, the hour is coming when you will not worship the Father on this mountain, or in Jerusalem. You do not know what you worship, but we know what we worship, because salvation comes from the Jews. But the hour is coming — it is here now — when those who worship truly will worship the Father in spirit and in truth. These are the worshipers the Father wants. God is a Spirit, and those who worship him must worship in spirit and in truth.

— John 4:10-24

And he told the woman that he was the Messiah, the one she had been waiting for. Jesus rejoiced that God had sent him to the poor and weak and despised, to Samaritans and widows and unrespectable people. Because of the singlemindedness of which simple people are capable, in their yearning for deliverance, they were more capable of recognizing him and the message of the Kingdom than more worldly and sophisticated people.

I thank you, Father, Lord of heaven and earth, because you have hidden these things from the wise and educated, and have revealed them to children; yes, that seemed good to you!

All things are given to me by my Father, and no one knows the Son but the Father, nor does anyone know the Father but the Son, and those to whom the Son reveals him. — Matthew 11:25-27

He said of the widow who dropped two tiny coins into the temple treasury:

I tell you, this poor widow has put in more than all of those who have put money into the treasury, because they gave from their great stores of riches, but she, poor as she is, has put in everything she has, her whole living! — Mark 12:43-44

Jesus was moved by the complete self-giving of the old woman. It was not the amount of money which pleased God, but the fullness of the gift. This wholeheartedness is asked of his followers. But possessions and vanity get in the way.

Who made me a judge or divider over you? Pay attention now, and beware of greed. A man's life is not found in the amount of property he owns. — Luke 12:14-15

When anyone asks you to a wedding, do not sit down in the place of highest honor. Someone higher than you might also have been invited, and your host might come and say to you, "Let this man sit here." Then you would go shamefully to the lowest place. When you are invited, take the lowest place. Then the host will say, "Friend, move to a higher place, where you can be honored by your fellow guests." Whoever lifts himself up will be moved down, and whoever humbles himself will be lifted up. — Luke 14:8-11

When you give a dinner, do not call your friends or brothers or family, or your prosperous neighbors. If you do they will pay back the invitation, and you will have your reward. When you give a feast, call the poor, the handicapped, the lame, the blind. Then you will be blessed, because they cannot reward you, and you will be rewarded when the just rise from the dead. — Luke 14:12-14

Jesus' followers were a close-knit group, and once were offended when they saw a man who was not of their company casting out demons in the name of Jesus.

Do not stop him. No one can do a miracle in my name, and easily speak evil of me. Whoever is not against us is on our side.

— Mark 9:39-40

Jesus asks his followers to be living signs of the Kingdom. The way they live together must reflect the reconciliation which they claim to believe in.

If your brother wrongs you, tell him that he has done so, privately. If he listens to you, you have your brother back again. But if he refuses to listen, then take one or two others with you, so that they may act as witnesses to what is said. If he refuses to listen to them, tell it to the church, and then if he refuses to listen to the church, he may be treated like a pagan or a tax collector.
I tell you, whatever you forbid on earth will be forbidden in heaven, and what you allow on earth will be allowed in heaven. Again I say, if two of you agree on earth about anything you wish to ask for, it will be done for you by my heavenly Father. Wherever two or three are gathered, I am there among them.

— Matthew 18:3-19

When Jesus asked his disciples who they thought he was, Peter answered, "You are the Messiah, the Son of the living God."

You are blessed, Simon, son of Jonah! Flesh and blood did not reveal this to you, but my Father in heaven. And I tell you: you are Peter. On this rock, I will build my church. The gates of hell will not close on it. I will give you the keys of the Kingdom, and whatever you forbid on earth will be forbidden in heaven, and what you allow on earth will be allowed in heaven.

— Matthew 16:18-19

Early Christian writers interpreted this to mean that the rock, the foundation of the church, was the confession of faith that Jesus is the Messiah, God's Son.

> If anyone wishes to be first, he must become the last, and be a servant to everyone.
>
> — Mark 9:33-35

> The Gentile kings lord it over their people, and those who exercise authority among them are called "benefactors".
> It will nòt be that way with you. The greatest among you must be like the youngest, and the chief must be a servant. For who is greater — the one who sits down to eat, or the servant? Certainly it is the one who sits to eat — but here I am with you, like a servant.
> You are the ones who stood by me during my tribulations. Now I give you the Kingdom my Father has given to me. You will eat and drink at my table in my Kingdom, and sit on thrones to judge the twelve tribes of Israel.
> Simon, Simon, Satan wants to have his way with all of you, sifting you like wheat. But I have prayed that your faith will not fail; and when you have become strong again, give strength to your brothers.
>
> — Luke 22:25-32

The authority which Jesus gave his church was an authority which shows itself in humility and service. When at the last supper he took on the role of a servant, to wash the feet of his followers, Peter was shocked: "You will never wash my feet!" Then Jesus answered him, "If I do not wash you, you are not one of my companions." And Peter answered, "Then wash all of me, not only the feet!" Jesus explained his action:

> You do not now understand what I am doing, but you will understand later.
> A man who has bathed does not need to wash any further; he is completely clean. You also are clean — but not every one of you.
> Do you understand what I have done for you? You call me "Master" and "Lord", and rightly: that is what I am. Then if I, your Lord and Master, have washed your feet, you should also wash one another's feet. I have given you an example; you should do what I have done to you.
> What I say is true: the servant is not greater than the one who sent him. If you know these things, you will be happy to do them.
> I do not speak of all of you; I know those I chose. But scripture must be fulfilled: "He who eats bread with me has lifted his heel against

me." I tell you this before it comes to pass, so that when it happens you may believe that I am what I said I am.

Truly, I tell you, he who receives whoever I send receives me, and he who receives me receives the one who sent me. — John 13:7-20

We are to be Christ to others. To strengthen us for the work, and to allow us to continue celebrating his presence among us, Jesus gave us the eucharist on the night before he died.

Go into the city, and say to the man I send you to, "The Master says my time is here. I will keep the Passover at your house, with my disciples." — Matthew 26:18

How I have longed to eat this Passover meal with you before I suffer! For I tell you, I will never eat it again, until it is all fulfilled in the Kingdom of God.

Take this, and divide it among yourselves. I tell you, I will not drink of the fruit of the vine until the Kingdom of God comes.

This is my body which is given for you: do this in memory of me.

This cup is the new covenant, shown in the blood I shed for you.

— Luke 22:15-20

The Passover blessing was customarily pronounced by the host as he distributed the bread; the third cup of wine was called "the cup of blessing." In celebrating the eucharist we not only celebrate the presence of Jesus among us. We look forward to the fulfillment of the Kingdom at the end of time. We bring that Kingdom into reality by being his people, and living out the consequences of what he has done for us. He loved us so much that he was willing to die for that love; when we are truly sorry he forgives us everything; he was a servant to all of the human race. He asks us to live this life — his life — in the world today, and gives us the strength to do it. It is the strength of the Spirit of God.

Peace be to you. As my Father sent me, so I send you.

Receive the Holy Spirit. Whose sins you forgive, are forgiven. Whose sins you leave unforgiven, are unforgiven. — John 20:22-23

All power on heaven and earth has been given to me. Therefore, go — teach all nations, baptizing them in the name of the Father, and of the Son, and of the Holy Spirit.

Teach them to do the things I have commanded.

Behold, I am always with you, even until the end of the world.

— Matthew 28:18-20